OCEAN

OCEAN

PHOTOGRAPHS FROM THE WORLD'S GREATEST UNDERWATER PHOTOGRAPHERS

Boyce Thorne-Miller,
Co-Founder of Ocean Advocates

Foreword by Sylvia A. Earle

Photography Editor James Gritz

A Richard Ballantine/Byron Preiss Book

CollinsPublishersSanFrancisco
A Division of HarperCollinsPublishers

First published in the USA 1993 by Collins Publishers
San Francisco
1160 Battery Street, San Francisco, CA 94111

Produced by Byron Preiss/Richard Ballantine, Inc.

Editor: Richard Ballantine
Captions/Interviews: Brendan Healey
Photography Editor: James Gritz
Book & Cover Design: Fearn Cutler
Special thanks to Ian Ballantine, Maura Carey Damacion,
Tony Koltz, Byron Preiss, Lena Tabori.

Endpapers Photograph by Burt Jones & Maurine Shimlock
Half-Title Photograph by David Hall
Title Page Photograph by Scott Frier
Copyright Page Photograph by Alex Kirkbride

Library of Congress Cataloging-in-Publication Data:

Thorne-Miller, Boyce
    Ocean: photographs from the world's greatest
underwater photographers / Boyce Thorne-Miller; foreword
by Sylvia A. Earle; photography editor, James Gritz.
        p.   cm.
    Includes index.
    ISBN 0-00-255156-X
    1. Marine biology. 2. Ocean. 3. Marine biology—
Pictorial works. 4. Ocean—Pictorial works. 5. Underwater
photography. I. Gritz, James. II. Title.
QH91.T46 1993
574.92—dc20   93-13238
                                                  CIP

Printed in Italy
10 9 8 7 6 5 4 3 2 1

CONTENTS

FOREWORD: EXPLORING THE OCEAN
By Sylvia A. Earle

Rapid changes are occurring in the ocean as the result of the actions of one species—humans. It is increasingly clear that the future of our kind depends on our learning how to live compatibly with the rest of life on Earth. In recent years, this need for "peaceful coexistence" has enhanced my enthusiasm for exploring the ocean—already high as a consequence of the thousands of mind-stretching dives I've taken as a marine scientist.

Since most of life on Earth is aquatic, in terms of both diversity and biomass, it seems reasonable that attention should be focused on getting to know who's who in the sea, and on understanding the ways that living creatures affect the character of the liquid systems that in turn influence the atmosphere, the weather, the climate, the very nature of the planet as a place hospitable to life.

In recent decades, in tandem with well-publicized efforts to probe the skies above, largely unheralded but stunning new discoveries have been made and new insights gained regarding the nature of this planet from the inside out. One of Earth's major geological formations was discovered during the 1950s: 25,000 miles of underwater mountain ranges running the length of the Atlantic, Pacific, and Indian oceans. Knowledge of plate tectonics, the movement of continents, seafloor spreading, the existence of hot, mineral-laden springs in the deep sea, and entire communities of life—and life-styles—previously unsuspected are among the discoveries that have caused many a textbook to be rewritten and new volumes to be composed.

It was only thirty-odd years ago that the existence of life in the deepest part of the ocean—36,000 feet down—was confirmed when, in 1960, the deep-diving bathyscaphe *Trieste* transported two men to the bottom of the Marianas Trench in the western Pacific. They peered out of the single, small porthole and saw eyes looking back. A small flounderlike fish gazed at them, probably as astonished by the presence of a huge submersible as the men inside were to see a familiar form of life in a space where pressure exerted is about 16,000 pounds per square inch, where there is no light, and where the water temperature is near freezing all the time.

Those who imagine that we now know all that is important to know about this planet should reflect on the fact that less than one-tenth of 1 percent of the deep sea—the area below convenient diving depth—has been explored. Mapped, yes. Seen, studied, researched, understood? No.

A few years ago, I listened to a famous mountain climber describe his recent ascent to the "last unclimbed high mountain peak on Earth." This great explorer said that he felt compassion for those following who had no new mountains to conquer, that the great era of exploration of Earth was over. This is a common misperception, one that starts at sea level and goes upward. Looking downward, into the ocean, it is clear that most of the mountain *ranges* have yet to be explored, and most of the mountains within them have yet to be seen, let alone climbed. Many have been mapped using acoustic scanners; a few have been glimpsed with special cameras or have had small samples taken from them by instruments lowered from the decks of ships; but, for most, exploration awaits. Perhaps the greatest discovery about the sea in our time may be the realization of the magnitude of our ignorance.

True, in recent years, ships, satellites, the space shuttle, and increasingly sophisticated instruments have helped provide information about the configuration of the seafloor, and about temperature, salinity, and the general physical and chemical composition of surface waters and their movements. But,

Sylvia Earle in the JIM diving suit off Hawaii. In 1979, Earle made the deepest untethered solo dive ever, to a depth of 1,250 feet. Hawaii. Chuck Nicklin.

as this book so eloquently shows, the ocean consists of more than rocks and water. From its glittering surface to its greatest depths, it is filled with life.

Scientists who have sought to estimate the number of fish in any given area—and perhaps to find out what *kinds* of fish are there and maybe even what they are doing—are keenly aware of the difficulties of studying even one aspect of this universe. To get a sense of the problems ocean explorers face, think for a moment of trying to learn about the life and customs of a foreign city by flying over it on a foggy day, blindly lowering nets and bottles and cameras to capture whatever might fortuitously appear in your path. A camera might spot a pedestrian or a bush or a bird; a net might snare a chunk of a building or a bicycle—but what could be determined about the real nature of life below?

Human beings, holding their breath, can stay submerged for only a short time—a minute or so. The deepest breath-hold dives have been to just beyond 300 feet, while breath-holding "working dives"—to explore or find food or salvage lost goods—tend to be to depths of less than 60 feet. Technology is the key to ocean access.

While sophisticated equipment is essential for full understanding, one aspect of the ocean is readily available to everyone, a few feet from any shore. Using simple technology—mask, fins, and snorkel—millions of people have witnessed the enormous diversity of life during excursions along the upper rim of an enormous arena that averages 13,000 feet in depth. Even in shallow water it is possible to find seaweed, sponges, jellyfish, sea squirts, urchins, bryozoans, polychaete worms, crabs, fish, and much more.

One of the ocean's most intriguing forms of life, gelatinous organisms called ctenophores, often live just under the surface, but many live only in the deep sea. Peering at them through a face mask or catching sight of them while cruising along in deep-diving submersibles, I am enchanted by these diaphanous creatures, characterized by bands of cilia and rippling with rainbow colors. Part of the appeal

is aesthetic—their sheer beauty. But there is more. The role of these midwater travelers and other gelatinous forms is becoming recognized as highly significant in terms of the ebb and flow of energy in the water column. These fragile beauties do not survive in nets, nor in the fossil record. To know them, to see the manifestation of their precious genetic cargo, to gain insight into their role in the functioning of our planet, it is necessary to go where they live—and patiently watch.

Every year, hundreds of new forms of life are discovered in the sea, and it is certain that many more will be found. More than 90 percent of the area on Earth suitable for life is aquatic space, and only a small fraction of that space has been explored. Many explanations have been offered to account for the lag in ocean exploration. Some point out that human beings are terrestrial and don't like to get wet. Others half-jokingly suggest that people like to look up, not down. It is often noted that there has been no equivalent to the space race to stimulate development of underwater technology.

In any event, no vehicle currently in operation can make a round-trip journey to where the *Trieste* went, seven miles down, many years ago. Only five submersibles now exist that are capable of going down to about half that depth, to 19,600 feet. Japan's *Shinkai 6500*, the deepest-diving manned submersible, is joined in a world fleet by Russia's *Mir I* and *Mir II*, the French system's *Nautile*, and the U.S. Navy's sub *Sea Cliff*. Several unmanned, remotely operated, and autonomous vehicles can go as deep, and a system for access to 33,000 feet is being built in Japan. Use of these technological assets is revolutionizing our understanding of the sea.

Unmanned systems are often used where it is considered too risky to send divers or even manned subs. However, as one who has been there, I can say

Mertensia. *Ctenophores, also known as comb jellies, are found throughout the ocean, from the surface to the deep sea. Greenland Sea. Dr. George Matsumoto.*

overleaf: *Brittle stars on a gorgonian red coral. Fiji. David Hall.*

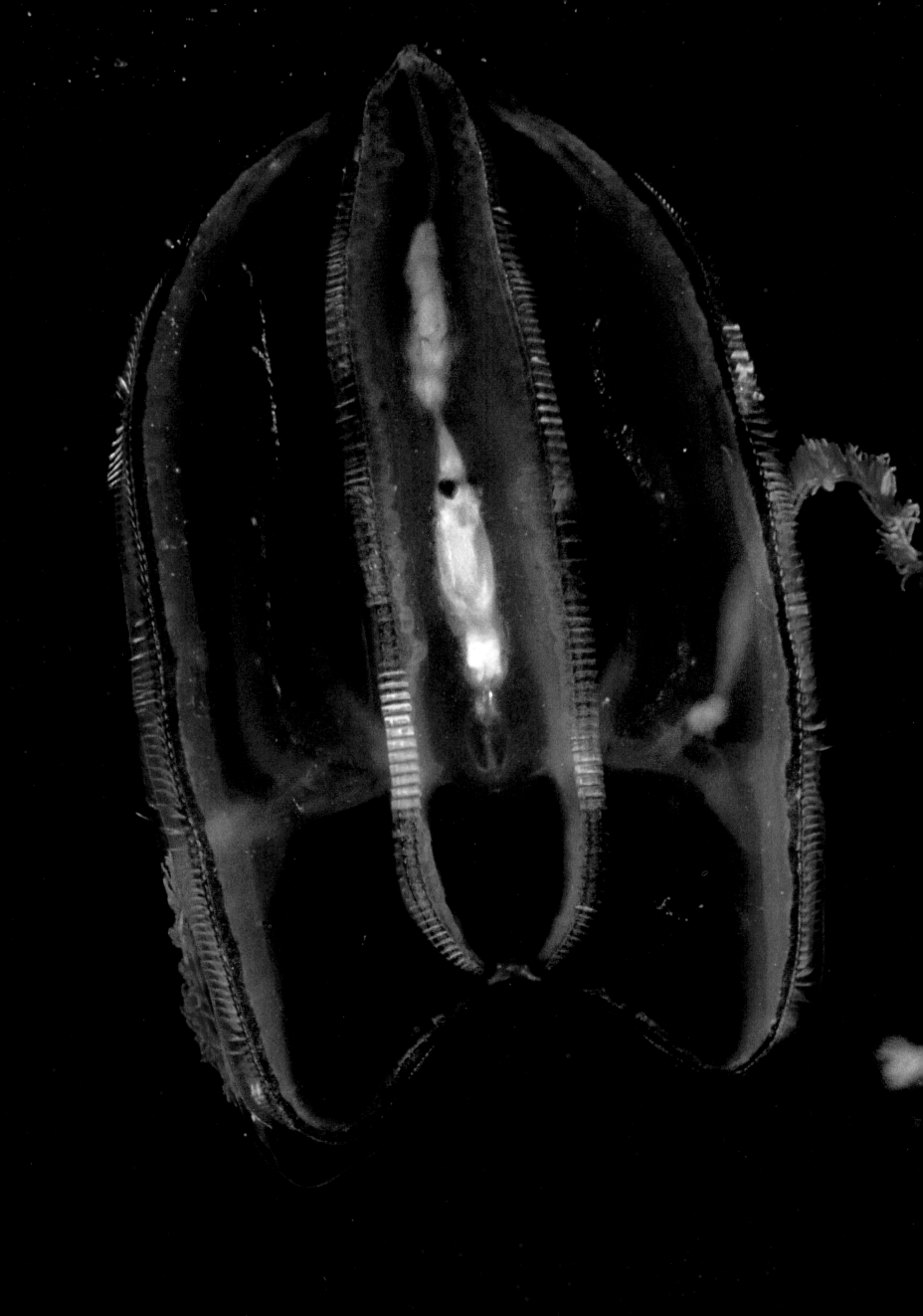

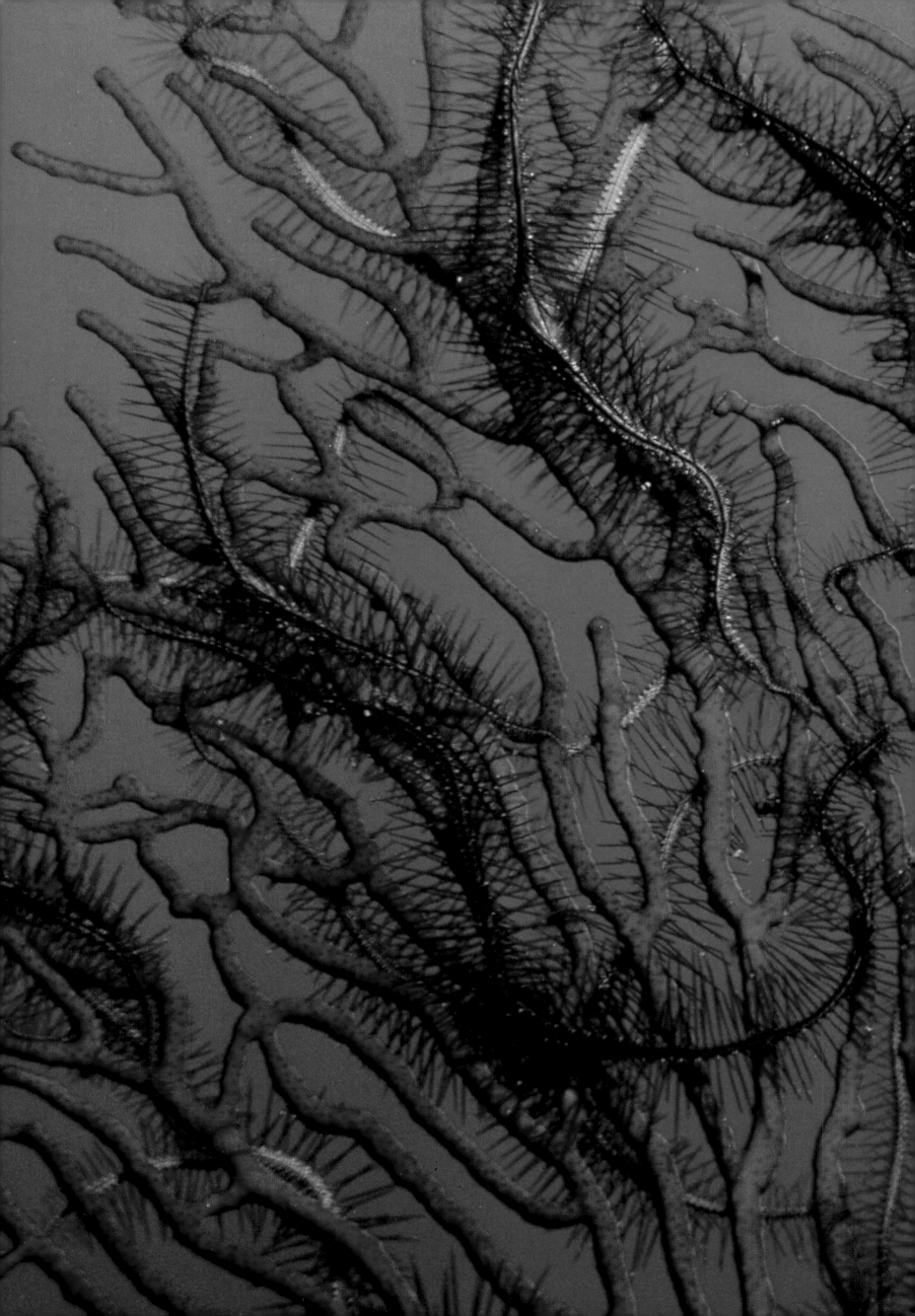

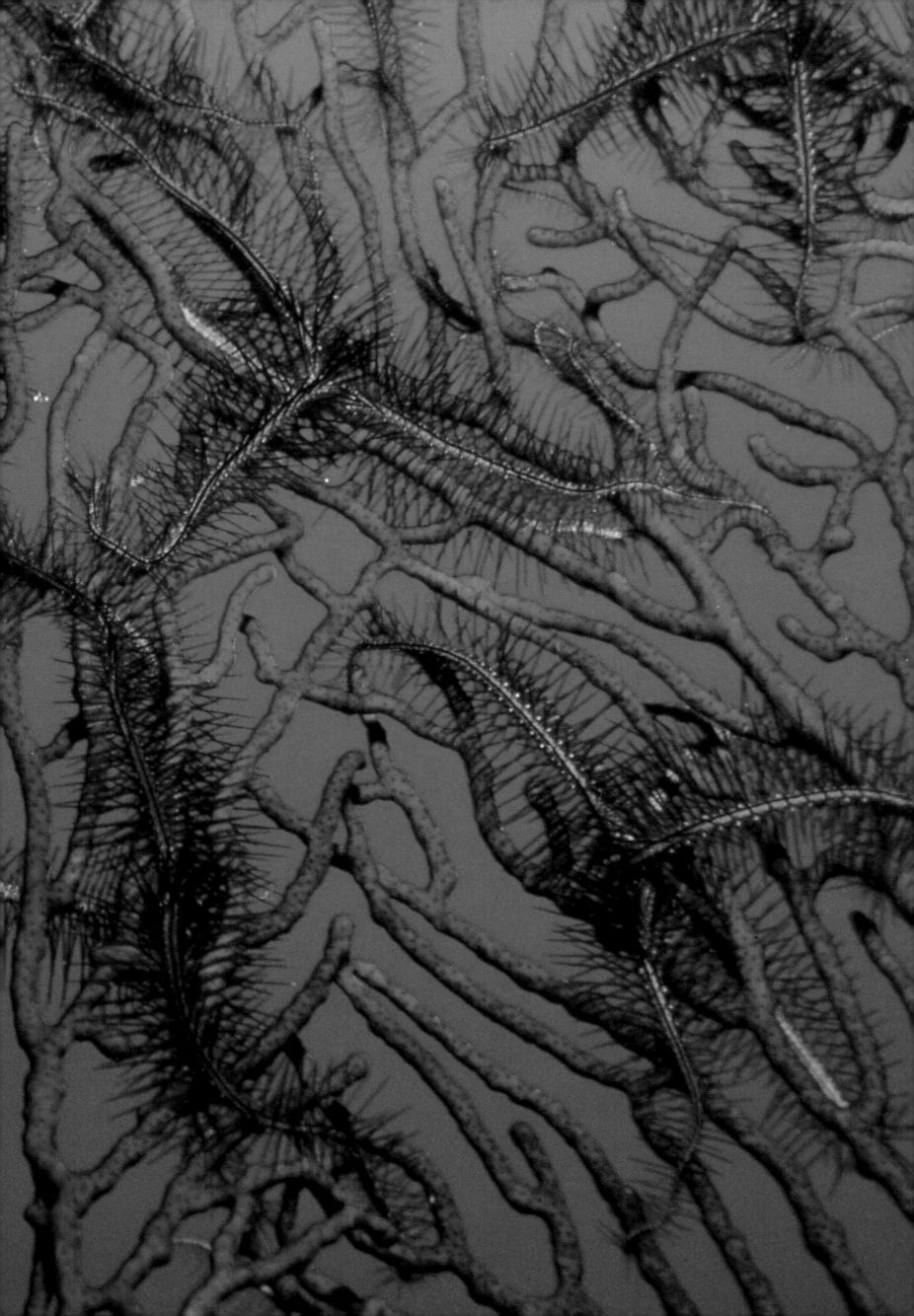

with certainty that there is *nothing* quite like being there. Remotely operated devices, although enormously useful in their own right, cannot wholly substitute for the human observer, whether viewing Earth from space or watching fish on a coral reef.

One setup that allows for more personal attention is the use of underwater habitats, in which observers live underwater for days or weeks, using the ocean as a laboratory in the same way that scientists on land work in the deserts or rain forests of their choice. About 50 underwater habitats have been used around the world, initially for scientific exploration and later for commercial and military applications.

In 1970, I joined three other scientists and an engineer during Project Tektite in the U.S. Virgin Islands for a two-week stay on the edge of a coral reef, 50 feet down. The pressure inside the Tektite underwater habitat was the same as the pressure outside, so diving time in the immediate area was essentially unlimited. It also made possible long excursions into the greater depths nearby.

For a while, my companions and I became resident aliens, and as such became a part of the ecosystem; we got up with the early-rising species and turned in after watching the changeover from day-active creatures to those that emerge mostly at night. I soon found landmarks that made the terrain as familiar as an above-water neighborhood, and I got to know fish not just as barracuda or angelfish, but as specific individuals recognizable by their distinctive appearance and behavior, and assigned them unscientific names such as Fang and Sweetlips.

Swimming at night was an ethereal experience. It is so easy to slip outside one's room on the reef into the dark sea when living *in* the sea. I always carried a flashlight, but often did not use it, allowing moon- and starlight to provide illumination to the subsea terrain, 50 to 130 feet below. With my light off, other lights were apparent—bioluminescence created by countless small creatures that sparkle, flash, and glow, usually in response to being touched. My human dive partners appeared sheathed in blue

silver as they moved, every turn of a flipper sending cascades of living sparks into a wake of blue fire. Such experiences are exhilarating, but they also provide insight into what it is like to be a living creature moving through a dark sea. Subtleties of behavior can be sensed, judgments made, memories provoked by the on-site presence.

Not everyone likes the idea of getting wet or staying submerged for days or weeks at a time, but it is increasingly easy and attractive to have life-changing experiences underwater—without getting wet. As a child, I longed for a bus that could travel into the sea, one with comfortable seats and large windows. Several dozen such buses, actually passenger submarines, now take people underwater in comfort and safety.

These systems, like most submarines, retain the same pressure as the pressure at sea level—one atmosphere—so no physical stress is experienced, even when the systems are submerged far beneath the surface. In recent years, the concept has been successfully applied to small "personal submersibles." I have had a chance to use a one-atmosphere system called JIM, named for the first person willing to try it. JIM resembles an astronaut suit, but, instead of being soft, it is hard, since it is made of metal to withstand increasing outside pressure while the inside pressure remains constant. Using JIM, I was able to descend into the twilight zone at 1,300 feet, six miles offshore from Makapuu Point on Oahu in Hawaii. In the clear tropical sea at midday, enough sunlight penetrated so that, without lights, I could see the ghostly shapes of sponges and soft corals on the seafloor, and watch small fish flit by with rows of lights gleaming from their silvery sides.

Another personal submersible, *Deep Rover*, makes it possible to go deeper, to 3,300 feet, where it is eternally dark except for the light provided by numerous small bioluminescent beings. *Deep Rover* does not look much like a diving suit, but in fact the

Red-and-black anemone fish. Fish have personalities and characteristic traits as distinct as those of many animals on land. Palau. David Hall.

submersible's mechanical arms serve as sensitive extensions of the pilot's own arms and hands, and subtle arm movements translate through micro-switches to achieve effortless propulsion.

Descending in *Deep Rover* along a steep dropoff in the Bahamas provided me with more opportunities to view the history of the planet—live. Many deep-sea animals belong to groups that are well represented in the fossil record but have few living representatives. A small fleet of squids darted by, and I was reminded of their long-deceased relatives, the ammonites. Until 65 million years ago, the sea hosted huge numbers of these spiral-shelled mollusks, but they and many others did not survive. Only about 300 kinds of octopuses and squids now live in the world's oceans. Each carries unique genetic codes that have persisted through hundreds of millions of years. All are vulnerable to the two aspects of human behavior that most influence the nature of the sea: what we put into the sea and what we take out.

Some species of squid apparently have small populations, while others occur in huge numbers and are vital as "cornerstone" species in ocean ecosystems. In Antarctica, millions of years of trial and error have led to systems dependent on the interactions among squids and seals, squids and birds, squids and fish, squids and whales, and, certainly squids and squids. The equation did not include human predation until quite recently, geologically speaking. Suddenly, millions of tons of squid are being taken away for fertilizer or food for humans, farm animals, and pets. What will be the consequences? We do not know how the removal of such enormous quantities of squid will affect the future of the squid species involved, or the future of the numerous creatures that have no alternatives about what to eat—or, ultimately, what the changes may mean to the future of mankind.

Squid are also vulnerable to things that are deliberately or inadvertently put into the sea. Hard trash is sometimes hazardous to sea creatures, but far more dangerous are the changes in the chemistry of the ocean brought about by the effluent of human activities. The impact of intentional dumping, as well as runoff from the land via streams and rivers, is most obvious in coastal waters, but ultimately the entire ocean system is affected.

There was a time, not long ago, when the often-used phrase "The solution to pollution is dilution" seemed to have some merit, when the sea appeared infinitely capable of absorbing whatever human beings put there. Until recently, it has seemed to some that the sea might also provide a never-ending supply of whales, fish, and other living resources. The recent precipitous decline of dozens of once-abundant species is evidence that there have been some serious miscalculations, about how much can be taken out of—and about the kind and amount of what can safely be put into—the sea.

I am not a doomsday scientist, suggesting that the end of Earth is imminent. Rather, as a dedicated planet-watcher, I am curious about what is happening to Earth's ecosystems, knowing that changes are being stimulated by rapidly expanding human activity—activity that has been concentrated in the span of my lifetime. Half a century is a minuscule amount of time in the 4.6-billion-year history of the planet, yet the impact of changes set in motion by humans during this short period may be on a scale with catastrophic events that occurred 65 million years ago during which the dinosaurs and many other species perished, perhaps as a result of volcanic activity or by large meteorites striking Earth.

Humankind is responsible for a current huge loss in species diversity and for the elimination of once-but-never-more ecosystems that took millennia to evolve. Our activities are linked to the widening

Many commercial fishing methods are indiscriminate.
right: *Shark caught in a gill net. Gill netting destroys bottom habitat and is nonselective in what it catches. California. Howard Hall.*

overleaf: *Seal trapped in a drift net. Drift nets can be up to 40 miles long. Drift netting has been called strip-mining of the seas, and, as this dead seal (which will certainly be discarded) shows, it is a remarkably wasteful method of harvesting seafood. Galápagos. Wes Walker.*

holes in Earth's ozone layer. We may be accelerating global warming, and certainly we are responsible for introducing toxic materials into the planet's life-support system—the air, land, and sea, and the living matrix that sets this planet apart from others and causes Earth to be hospitable to our kind.

There are no quick-fix answers to the questions about what to do, but one action stands out as necessary: to embrace the planet's remaining environmental capital, its natural wilderness, and protect it absolutely. Our lives depend on maintaining Earth's remaining healthy ecosystems. In the case of the oceans, several coastal marine parks, preserves, sanctuaries, estuarine research reserves, and wildlife habitat reserves have been established that will help serve this end, but little has been done to ensure the good health of the open ocean or deep sea beyond national jurisdictions.

Hours spent observing life in the oceans have provoked reflection about how long those systems were in the making and how swiftly they can be altered or eliminated. Everywhere, I encounter descendants of microorganisms that were on Earth two billion years ago. Half a billion years ago, there were sponges and jellyfish and horseshoe crabs and numerous other creatures whose modern counterparts still populate the seas. Cruising around in deep-sea wilderness areas, admiring such creatures, I am mindful that my species must be regarded as a "newcomer," with recognizable ancestors apparent in only the last few million years. Civilization began roughly at the end of the last ice age, about 10,000 years ago. I cannot help but wonder how long descendants of humankind will reside on Earth. Can we weather the present changes and emerge as successful partners with the rest of life on Earth, not

consuming in one century the means for a successful future? Can we hope to have a future as bright as the distinguished track record of certain dinosaurs? Will ours be one of those resilient species that maintain a place on the planet for 30 million years? Or might we even be able to maintain a timeline as distinguished as that of modern coelacanths, a kind of fish that appears little changed in 300 million years?

Clearly, the pressures on planetary systems are increasing; the size of the planet is not. If we are wise, and not just clever, perhaps our descendants will celebrate this era as one when those now alive looked around, took stock, and decided to give real thought to our future—and theirs.

The fossil ammonite (left) and "living fossil" chambered nautilus (above). The chambered nautilus is the only living representative of a large group of nautiloids that were dominant 400 to 500 million years ago. Related ammonoids, like the fossil ammonite, dominated the seas 65 to 250 million years ago, but none have survived. Both ammonoids and nautiloids are cephalopods, related to modern-day octopuses and squid. The chambered nautilus, like the ammonites, has an outer shell, but in octopuses and squid this shell is smaller and internal.
left: *South Dakota. Thomas Wiewandt.*

above: *Papua New Guinea. Amos Nachoum.*

overleaf: *Baby green sea turtles. Suriname. Frans Lanting.*

JEAN-MICHEL COUSTEAU

Executive Vice President of The Cousteau Society

As a child, I looked out on the Mediterranean Sea from my window. It was my front yard and I sensed even then that it was my father's office, his playground, and his mistress. When I was seven years old, my father very gently introduced my mother, my brother, and me to the world under water using the scuba system he co-invented. So the sea became a part of me in a way that is like second nature. I miss it when I'm away from it as you miss the presence of a friend.

Most of us experience the strong bond that is natural between humans and the ocean. Look how we line the shores and long for a glimpse of the sea. In the United States for example, something like 80 percent of the population lives within a hundred miles of the coast. Everyone is linked to the ocean in one way or another. Rocky Mountain snowcaps, for example, are frozen ocean. Rains that soak Kansas corn are driven by the climate-regulating machinery of the ocean—which redistributes heat in its myriad currents like an immense global circulatory system. It's a universal dynamic in our lives.

A few years ago, I was diving in California near Anacapa Island off the coast of Santa Barbara. I felt someone scratch my head, and I thought I was being teased by my dive buddy. But when I looked around my dive buddy was 20 feet away. Then I looked up and saw a large, spotted harbor seal, wide-eyed and whiskered, a foot above me, staring intently. It had come to inspect my gray hair. We stared at each other. Later, I couldn't help but think of its long evolutionary history from a sea creature to a land creature, then back to the sea, a route the whales, the dolphins—all the marine mammals—took millions of years ago. For a moment, I envied my flippered friend the route his ancestors had taken.

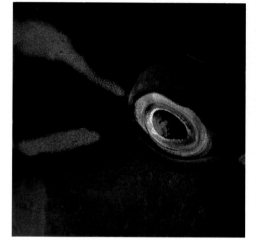

Parrotfish eye. Red Sea.
Burt Jones & Maurine Shimlock.

My love of the ocean took me into the field of architecture. When I was 15 years old, my father was constructing underwater habitats, and I wanted to design fabulous submarine structures to house cities of the future. I became a marine architect before I had to accept that it was a beautiful dream but not a practical one. I realized there was no reason for large numbers of people to live underwater. Accepting that I was ultimately land-bound made my time at sea even more valuable.

What is very difficult to accept is that although the ocean is an intricate part of my life and my character, I can no longer take it for granted. I feel personally at risk. I worry because we are using the sea as the universal sewer. The ocean covers 72 percent of the planet's surface, but the area that's most important, the area where we find the most life, is the narrow coastal shelf. It's only 4 percent of the ocean's surface but it's where we put the most pressure with our dumping, building, reshaping, fishing. As a result of man's use of fossil fuels, a thin layer of oil now covers most of the ocean's surface, choking the microscopic life that is the base of the food chain, changing life at the most basic level. We have very little time to reverse what we have been doing and minimize our effect not just on the ocean but on the entire natural system. It's quite frightening.

My work with the Cousteau Society has been one way of trying to give back to the sea. My experience has been so rich—how could I do anything less? And the consequences of not acting are too great. We need, all of us, to be responsible for our effect on the sea, the source of life on Earth. My main goal is to continue to show the beauty of the ocean to everyone because I know that ultimately "people will protect what they love."

Butterfly fish. Jean-Michel Cousteau has long enjoyed the beauty of the ocean and worked to protect it.
Red Sea. Chris Newbert.

TED DANSON

Actor and President of American Oceans Campaign

The roots of my efforts to protect the ocean are easy to trace. One day, my wife Casey and I were walking with our children along the beach and came across a sign that said Water Polluted: No Swimming. When you try to describe to your child why this is so, you come up lacking. It was then that I decided to do something about protecting the ocean.

Many other factors played a role. My parents had a lot to do with my interest in the environment as did Robert Sulnick. He is now executive director of American Oceans Campaign, but at that time he was president of an organization called No Oil, which was fighting Occidental Petroleum's plan to drill sixty oil wells off Pacific Palisades. At that point, Casey and I said, "Why don't we put all our time, money, and energy into one area that can generate some positive results?" and so we created American Oceans Campaign.

We weren't entirely sure of where to direct our energies when we started AOC, though, so we went to the Scripps Institution of Oceanography and asked for an unbiased assessment of the ocean's problems. They told us that coastal pollution is the main hazard. It's not the sexiest issue, but it certainly is the most pressing.

When you walk the beach in a place like Santa Monica, you see a beautiful ocean, but what is underneath the surface is kind of spooky. Over the years, we have dumped many things into the ocean that we thought the ocean could handle but that we have found to be highly toxic. Most of the household products that we use eventually wind up in the ocean. With so many households using toxic products—plus all the other things that have been dumped illegally—the ocean is a toxic cocktail.

Everything that we do on land ends up affecting coastal waters, and these areas are most important. The coastal waters are nurseries for marine life. Without healthy coastal waters, we would soon have aquatic deserts as opposed to oceans teeming with life. We should work to keep coastal areas healthy for all marine life; instead, we are poisoning our coasts and directly damaging our food chain. What we need to do is address the issue of toxins at the source and learn how to use alternative products.

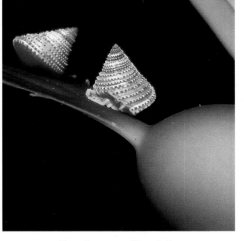

Jewel-top snail on kelp.
California. Norbert Wu.

If you want to help the oceans, you must make your voice heard in the political arena. People should write to their local congressmen or congresswomen and demand stronger legislation to govern our waters. They must also clean up their own households. All that stuff under the sink is highly toxic. It can be replaced by nontoxic, biodegradable products that don't poison our environment. We must start thinking about the problems our oceans face—long range. And we must think about what condition the ocean will be in if we don't start now to change our ways. What will we be leaving our children?

I truly believe that we are all beginning to wake up and are seeing what has to be done. I know that it will be a long, hard job, but it certainly is worth it. Let's give back what our oceans have given us!

American Oceans Campaign, which Ted Danson co-founded with Robert Sulnick, concentrates on issues of coastal conservation. Among other accomplishments, AOC participated in the coalition that successfully protected Alaska's Arctic National Wildlife Refuge from oil development, helped bring about the banning of drift nets in American coastal waters, and drafted the first-ever beach protocol for Los Angeles County. Washington. Nancy Sefton.

Chapter One
THE LIVING OCEAN

Seen from space, Earth is blue—the blue of the one great ocean that covers most of the globe—for Earth is not a land planet, like Mars or Venus, but an ocean planet. The land that rises above the sea occupies less than 30 percent of Earth's total area. In fact, when the planet is seen from a distance, the continents seem scarcely more than very large islands.

Mars and Venus differ from Earth in another essential way: they are dead worlds. Earth is the only planet in the solar system that supports life. And it is able to support life because of the ocean. For the ocean is our cradle, the regulator of our life-supporting atmosphere, and the key to continuing life on the planet.

Life began in the ocean more than 3 billion years ago. Within the ocean waters living things prospered and multiplied. Not until some 2.5 billion years later did life invade dry land, as species evolved to adapt to the land's harsher environments. The coming of the dinosaurs, of mammals, and of humans, the splendid variety of plants, animals, and birds—all of the important events of life on land span barely 15 percent of the total time of living things on Earth.

Today, the land abounds in many hundreds of highly-developed ecosystems and in a magnificent diversity of species, yet it is the ocean that contains more than 95 percent of our biosphere, the space on the planet where living things dwell. And it is the ocean that absorbs, stores, and releases the sun's energy, and thus controls our climate and makes the land habitable.

Until recently, the ocean had been a mysterious place to us, hostile and perilous. The sheer size

Orcas, commonly known as killer whales, are fearsome predators. Enormous, swift, and intelligent, orcas hunt and eat birds, fishes and squids, and large sea mammals, but have never been known to attack humans.
Alaska. Flip Nicklin.

of the ocean, the sweep and energy of the ocean's waves, tides, and currents, the great depths, and the exotic forms of the ocean's animal life have been aspects of an adversarial relationship between the ocean and humankind: man challenged, man against nature, man against the wild, destructive elemental powers.

In 1942, Jacques Cousteau developed the self-contained underwater breathing apparatus (scuba), and for the first time it became possible to venture underwater with some safety and freedom, and for a relatively long time. The ocean no longer seemed completely hostile to humankind. In fact, it seemed almost hospitable.

To experience a tiny corner of the living ocean—by diving among coral reefs, for instance—is at once exhilarating and startling. It is a sudden exposure to a complex and splendorous world of creatures, almost all of which appear to be very unlike anything one meets on land. They are different because their shapes are suited to movement in

aqueous surroundings. And their colors relate to their social behavior, feeding and defense behavior, and habitat. For many of us, diving in their world is an emotional and intellectual revelation. For some, the experience is deeper: religious or mystical. Fear and alienation are replaced by wonder and love; a keen awareness of life all around, life of which we are part.

Coral reefs are colorful and dynamic, yet they are only a small part of the marine environment. If only we could see beyond the shallow coasts, out across the continental shelves, down the great slopes

right: *Diver with giant jellyfish. Jellyfish are poor swimmers, but they can move by pulsating their bell bodies. They capture prey when it contacts their tentacles. The tentacles, which trail from the jellyfish's bell body, have stinging nematocysts, small barbs that release upon contact with prey and immobilize or kill it. California. Howard Hall.*

below: *Pacific manta ray. The diver is holding on to a pair of remoras, pilot fish that have attached themselves to the ray. The manta ray is also known as the devilfish, because of the large horn-like flaps protruding from its head. Sea of Cortez. Howard Hall.*

into the deep abyss, and then up from the deep abyss to the surface of the open ocean! If only, in a swift journey through the ocean, we were able to call upon microscopic and telescopic vision at will, and view all the different kinds of life supported by the ocean: from the giant whales to the teeming microbes, from the streamlined tuna to the delicately beautiful nudibranch, from the star-spangled surface waters where plankton cells flash bits of stored-up sunlight to the elaborate glowing patterns on bizarre deep-sea fish!

We can, in part. We are beginning to do some of these things, but slowly and with great difficulty. Deep-diving submersibles enable us to explore the ocean depths, while advances in camera and film technology allow us to record our findings. Progress in sampling techniques, biochemistry, and microscopy has expanded our ability to find and identify deep-sea life.

The discoveries made during these explorations into the deep are remarkable, as are the permanent images the explorers have brought us of what they have found: life-forms that remained in the sea when living things first crept onto land half a billion years ago, and weird creatures living in conditions we thought were impossible for life. These revelations are changing our ideas not only about the extent of life on Earth but about the role of the oceans in maintaining that life. Yet we are only at the beginning of such revelations. To date, we have seen less than 1 percent of the deep seafloor, and the thousands upon thousands of cubic miles of water above it teem with life about which we know little.

The ocean that is the source of life is also a vast frontier.

right: *Painted tunicate on a gorgonian coral. Tunicates, also known as "sea squirts," are primitive invertebrate animals and early ancestors of vertebrates. They are called tunicates because their bodies are enclosed in durable "tunics"—cloaks reinforced with cellulose.*
Bahamas. Doug Perrine.

below: *A trip in a submersible off Grand Cayman shows tourists that the ocean supports a variety of different life-forms and therefore deserves protection.*
Grand Cayman. Courtney Platt.

OCEAN GEOGRAPHY

The geographical boundaries we are used to on land tend to be definite and relatively stable: mountain ranges, rivers, plains, deserts, and, of course, seacoasts. But the ocean is not an area, like the land; it is a volume, filled with a fluid in dynamic motion. Consequently, although some of the ocean's boundaries are relatively definite and stable—the seafloor and the edges of land—others are "soft." The "soft" boundaries exist within the dynamic volume of water, while the hard boundaries can be found where fluid water meets solid earth—along the coast and the seafloor.

When the continental coastline drops below the ocean surface, the seafloor then slopes outward for many miles before dropping sharply, to a depth of 9,000 feet or more. The relatively flat, sometimes undulating margin bordering the continents, known as the continental shelf, is covered mostly with sand or mud. But in some places this gentle landscape is interrupted by rocky outcroppings or by areas where strong currents scour a gravelly bottom.

At the outer edge of the continental shelf, some 200 to 1,500 feet (average 450) below the surface and anywhere from 20 to 200 (average 44) miles from shore, the seafloor takes a steep plunge to the abyssal plain. The great "bluffs" that connect the continents with the abyss tend to be much more physically unstable than the seafloor above and below. Powerful boundary currents may sweep alongside them, and there are frequent landslides. The abyssal plain itself, the vast expanse of deep ocean floor, is covered by thick, soft sediments and relatively slow-moving waters.

Cutting across continental shelves, slopes, and the abyssal plain are canyons and trenches with sharp, rocky sides. Swift currents flow through these

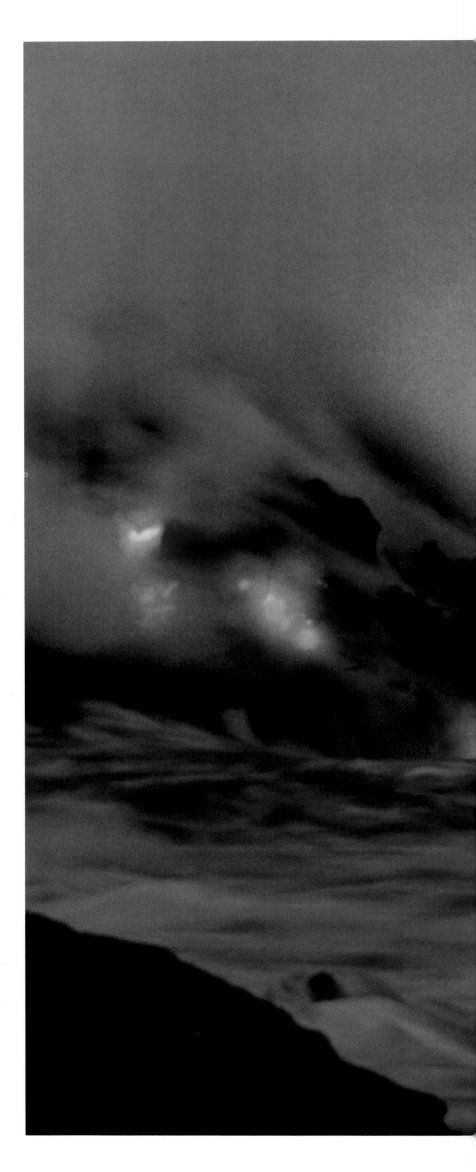

Kilauea Volcano, Hawaii, is one of the most active volcanoes on Earth. Most open-ocean islands were formed by volcanoes. Hawaii. James D. Watt.

above: *Christopher Columbus saw a sargassum swimming crab much like this one while en route to the New World and mistakenly assured his men that land must be near. The Sargasso Sea lies off the United States' Atlantic coast and beyond the Gulf Stream in the eye of a huge, circular ocean current. It is several thousand square miles in area and is dotted with floating masses of sargassum weed. This crab is only one of several kinds of unrelated animals that blend into the sargassum weed by mimicking its coloration. Florida. Doug Perrine.*

right: *Anchovies graze on plankton and are in turn consumed by humans, whales, dolphins, tuna, and birds. Anchovies are found in massive schools in near-shore, nutrient-rich habitats in all warm ocean waters throughout the world. British Virgin Islands. Al Grotell.*

great fissures. The deepest trenches plummet to the greatest depths of 6 or 7 miles.

Areas of water may be marked off by soft boundaries. These boundaries separate waters that differ markedly in temperature, salinity, nutrients, and/or light, and they are often defined by currents. The boundaries describe spaces—volumes—that support characteristic sea-life communities. Thus, in Earth's one ocean many distinct ecosystems exist, defined by both horizontal and vertical borders.

Marine ecosystems are characterized both by the physical conditions within them and by the kinds of biological communities they support. For example, a major upwelling—water rising from the bottom, to replace water moved away by surface currents—brings cool, nutrient-rich waters to the west coast of South America. These nutrients support luxuriant growths of phytoplankton, plants that float or drift with the movement of the sea. These in turn are consumed by zooplankton, the planktonic animals, which are eaten by small fish, such as anchovies, which are eaten by large predatory fish, such as tuna, and seabirds. Though the upwelling food chain is relatively short, and the number of species in the community relatively small, the productivity is high: this particular upwelling supports a tremendous fish population. The fishermen of Peru and Chile, for example, catch about five million tons of anchovies in a good year. It is by far the largest single-species fishery in the world.

Water in the ocean is always moving—sometimes swiftly, as it does along the western portions of the Gulf Stream, and sometimes sluggishly, as it does along the abyssal plain. Moving water links

coastal ecosystems with the open ocean, the bottom with the surface, the land with the sea, and continents and islands with one another. Turbulent seas and ocean streams, large and small, carry sediments and species from one location to another.

All this motion has two effects: things are carried about, including living organisms; and soft boundaries separating biologically distinctive communities are created by the currents. The result is a broad dispersal of many species; currents carry these species' reproductive stages (spores, eggs, and larvae) or even, for smaller animals and plants, their mature stages to other locations where they may—or may not—find favorable environments.

In addition to living organisms, the nutrients that support them are also transmitted by currents and turbulence. Carried along with these nutrients, of course, are toxic pollutants. Pollution from land, entering the ocean through purposeful discharge or accidental runoff, may cause widespread degradation of the marine environment.

above: Salp chain. Salp chains are colonies of primitive planktonic tunicates that have gelatinous bodies and drift with ocean currents. As larvae, salps have rudimentary brains and spinal cords that disappear when the salps mature and become adults. Salps develop into colonial chains by asexual budding. These chains can reach 60 feet in length.
California. Howard Hall.

right: Dolphins can swim faster than 35 miles per hour and cover long distances. Some have home ranges that are quite small (about 30 square miles), whereas others, especially open-ocean species, may range through territories of about 600 square miles.
Sea of Cortez. Norbert Wu.

overleaf: Mud crab. Montebello Islands, Australia.
David Doubilet.

The real theme of the ocean is interconnectedness. Its fluid nature provides for the broad distribution of many species and also results in the existence of fewer species than live on land. On dry land it is easier for particular gene pools to become isolated, and for new species to develop.

WHERE THE SEA
MEETS THE LAND

O f the many boundaries we can observe in the
ocean, the most dramatic, at least from a human
point of view, are those that define the meeting place
of sea and exposed land. The ocean pounds relent-
lessly against rocky sea cliffs; huge waves curl toward
sandy beaches; and low-lying coastal lands are inun-
dated with typhoon-driven seawater. The meeting of
earth and water beneath the ocean's surface is less
dynamic, but it is equally important if we consider
the tremendous multitude of living things that dwell
there.

While all oceanic life-forms are alike in being
continuously bathed in seawater, those living on the
intertidal shores of lands and continents—that is, on
the shores that lie between low and high tides—and
those that live farther out on the seafloor have in one
way or another adapted to that firm, or relatively
firm, subsurface of rock or sand or mud where they
make their homes. Unlike their free-floating or free-
swimming neighbors in the waters above and beyond,
these species anchor, dig, creep, crawl, slither, or in
some other way interact with the ocean bottom.

THE COASTS

The seacoasts of the world provide for a rich and
diverse abundance of ecosystems. Among the more
important and apparent of these are coastal wetlands,
beaches and mud flats, estuaries of various sorts,
reefs, intertidal rocky shores, and subtidal seaweed
beds.

The coastal zone is the bastion of seaweeds;
green, red, and brown algae that form the meadows,
forests, and bush of the coastal ocean. Hundreds of

*Low tide gives beachcombers a glimpse into the undersea world.
Here, in the water of a tide pool, anemones remain open and
ready to eat. Several sea stars congregate in the pool, while others
remain damp by huddling in crevasses. The seaweeds survive
exposure to air by retaining moisture or tolerating drying.
Olympic National Park, Washington. Thomas Wiewandt.*

species of algae line the richest rocky shores, many of them dipping in and out of the water with the rising and falling of the tide. This is also the zone where shelled animals cling to rocks and graze on tender young seaweed; where starfish and crabs scour the bottom for food, living and dead; and where hermit crabs and barnacles, fiddler crabs and mud worms make their homes. Here also reside shellfish: clams, oysters, mussels, scallops, abalone, and other delicacies for our tables.

Sea lions easily make the transition from land to sea. They feed in the ocean on fish and squid, but they mate and give birth on land. These Stellar's sea lions are now protected from humans. Alaska. James Gritz.

The coastal zone itself represents, all told, only a minute portion of the ocean. Still, it plays a major part in the ecology of the ocean. For it is along the coasts that many animal species have their nursery grounds. It is also where nutrients—and toxins—enter the ocean from the land.

Although it has a blue sheen, this seaweed is a brown algae that is iridescent because it contains refractive oil. There are three major divisions of macroalgae—red, green, and brown—distinguished by the pigments they use to capture light for photosynthesis. Algae need several pigments to enable them to more efficiently use the limited light that penetrates seawater.
Grand Cayman. Doug Perrine.
overleaf: *Penguins. Falkland Islands. Frans Lanting.*

THE SEAFLOOR

Beyond the shores, where the edge of the sea laps dry land, lie the plains and slopes, the plateaus and mountains, the canyons and trenches that make up the greater part of the ocean floor. These generally form a much less dramatic interface than the coastline does between the fluid ocean and the hard earth's crust.

Still, drama is to be found here, and sometimes even great spectacle. For shallow-water benthic (seafloor) communities include such noted zones of biological diversity as coral reefs, where even a casual diver observes a fantastic array of colors. Some fish flash prominent patterns of colors to attract mates or to warn competitors. Others, armed with rows of sharp teeth, are colored to blend with their surroundings; virtually invisible, they lie in wait for unsuspecting prey to wander by. Small crustaceans and fish busily clean the teeth and scales of larger fish, which are queued up and awaiting the service.

Less densely packed than coral reefs, the subtidal floors of continental shelves offer their own form of beauty, such as that found in the giant kelp forests. Deeper still, below the continental slopes and all across the vast abyssal plains, lies another very different and endlessly surprising world. For many years, ocean scientists believed that these places were empty deserts. But recent studies suggest a landscape alive with perhaps millions of species. These creatures are not, it seems, the huge monsters of science-fiction nightmares. Rather, they are often inconspicuous, even microscopic organisms, thinly spread over a vast area.

Six-banded grouper and fairy basslets over soft corals. Reefs are the rain forests of the ocean, in that they include a remarkable number of species and have a complex physical structure providing many different kinds of habitats for a variety of animals. Fiji. F. Stuart Westmorland.

above: *Twenty-arm starfish and orange bat starfish. Starfish, now becoming known as sea stars because they are not in fact fish, are a familiar sight on beaches because they often live in intertidal regions. Most species of sea stars have five arms, although some species have more than two dozen. As echinoderms (which means "spiny-skinned"), sea stars are related to sea urchins, sea cucumbers, feather stars, and sand dollars, among others. Echinoderms have never developed heads despite their relatively high position on the evolutionary ladder.*
Monterey Bay, California. James Gritz.

right: *Giant kelp require sunlight for photosynthesis, cool water currents for nutrients, and a rocky bottom for anchoring. The giant kelp is the world's largest alga and grows to more than 100 feet long. The plants are anchored to the bottom by "holdfasts," rootlike structures that attach themselves to the rocks but do not take in nutrients and water as a land plant's roots do. The kelp forests off the coast of California are home to a variety of animals, including abalone, rockfish, and otters.*
Monterey Peninsula, California. Steve Rosenberg.

WHERE THE SEA MEETS THE SKY

On the surface of the ocean, at the very point of its interface with the atmosphere, there is a kind of "skin," a layer about as thick as a human hair, which is a natural organic film formed by the strong surface tension of the water's outermost boundary. Within this skin, or microlayer, a multitude of both living and nonliving things are concentrated. The living community includes eggs and larvae of numerous species, such as fish and shellfish, that spend their adult lives elsewhere; phytoplankton, drifting microalgae, which congregate there because the light intensity is greatest and nutrients are plentiful; microscopic animals that feed on the phytoplankton; as well as bacteria. Nutrients and toxins also concentrate here. The particular physical characteristics of this skin are quite stable, enabling the microlayer to remain intact with its microscopic community "hanging in there," even in the face of strong winds and high waves. It constitutes a rich and important community of the sea.

Just beneath the microlayer, in the next few inches of the ocean, live animals that rely on the food these waters provide. Many other species, including larger crustaceans and jellyfish, come up from below to prey upon the microscopic life at the surface. The microlayer also provides food for creatures that live on the other side: seabirds from above dine on the rich broth.

The microlayer magnifies the toxic effects of water pollution. Metals in seawater bind to the organic molecules in the microlayer, and become more concentrated than in the waters beneath. Some metals, such as iron, are useful as nutrients, but others, such as cadmium and lead, are toxic. Many pollutants from human activities, instead of dissipating

Dolphins are among the sea creatures that make the transition between sea and air. They have to surface to breathe, and often they leap into the air in play.
Oahu, Hawaii. David Doubilet.

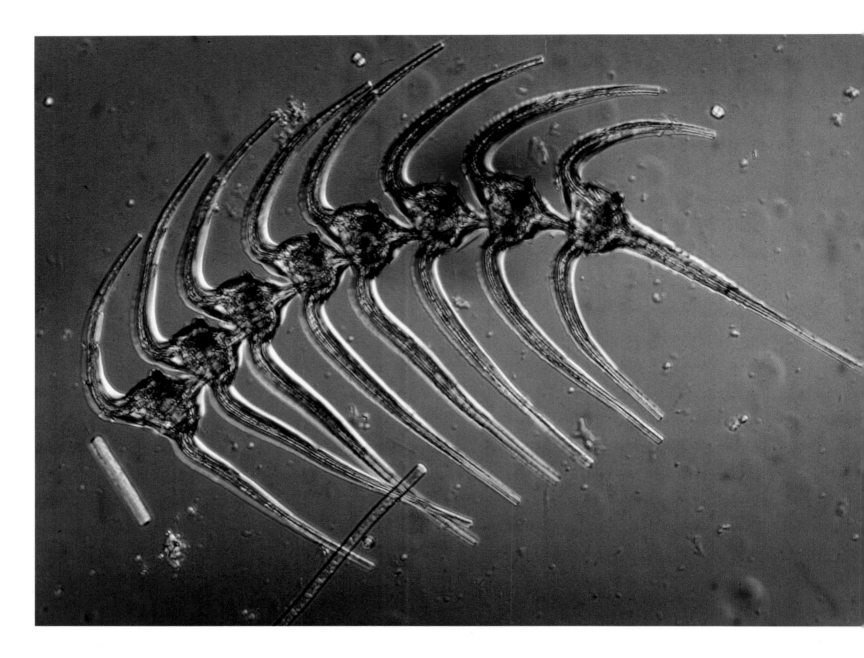

above: Ceratium vultur. *This is a colonial chain-forming dinoflagellate common in tropical waters. Dinoflagellates are single-celled microalgae that are planktonic—drifting with currents—but can also swim by moving their flagella, threadlike appendages that propel them through the water with a spiraling motion. Often found in the microlayer and sunlit waters beneath, dinoflagellates both photosynthesize and consume organic material. These are characteristics of both plants and animals, so it is difficult to classify dinoflagellates as either. They are generally considered to be plants because photosynthesis is their primary source of energy. Caribbean. Paul Hargraves.*

throughout the entire ocean, become concentrated within the microlayer, and enter the food chain.

The biological community near the ocean surface is not only vital to the food chain; it may also be critical in regulating climate change. The exchange between the ocean and the air plays a significant role in determining the composition of Earth's atmosphere.

The carbon dioxide content of the atmosphere can cause significant climate changes. The microplants in the surface layer take up carbon dioxide in photosynthesis and incorporate it into plant tissue. Some of that material ultimately sinks to the bottom of the ocean, where it remains until the slow process of deep-sea bacterial decomposition releases the carbon dioxide back into the water. Over very long, geologic time periods, some of this carbon dioxide is taken up out of the system, stored in calcium carbonate shells and the calcareous skeletons of

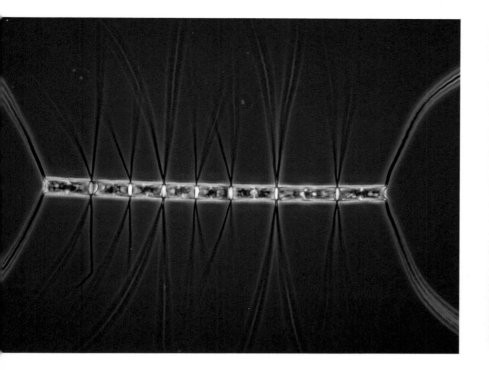

marine animals, such as corals and some algae. The rate at which each of these biological pumps works can critically affect the atmospheric concentration of carbon dioxide. And this in turn affects average global temperatures.

Both abundance and species of the phytoplankton are important in this process. For instance, among the phytoplankton that populate the open ocean, there are beautiful microscopic species with decorative calcium carbonate plates on their cell walls. Increases in the populations of these plants could increase the ocean's intake of carbon dioxide from the atmosphere. In time, this could counteract other sources of carbon dioxide entering the Earth's atmosphere.

Another type of microplant in the surface layer has a similar effect on climate, but for different reasons. These plants release a sulfide gas that bubbles into the atmosphere, where it acts as an effective seed for cloud formation. Warmer temperatures favor the growth of sulfide-gas-producing plants in northern seas, so it is projected that increased cloud formation and cooling may counterbalance the current global warming trend caused by air pollution.

The microlayer is the site of biologically controlled exchanges of gases between the atmosphere and the ocean. The chemical state of the microlayer is critical to the functioning of that system, and pollution could have a severe effect on it.

above left: Chaetocerus affinis *is a colonial diatom. Diatoms are single-celled plants that comprise a major portion of the mass of phytoplankton. Each cell in the chain has two long spines, which link with spines on adjacent cells. This adaptation, in which individual cells are linked up into chains, provides more buoyancy than individual cells. Diatoms begin the food chain. Often they are eaten by copepods (tiny crustaceans related to shrimp and crabs), which are in turn eaten by small fish. A cubic foot of summer seawater can contain more than 12 million individual phytoplankton cells, most of them diatoms.*
Narragansett Bay, Rhode Island. Paul Hargraves.

above right: Chaetocerus debilis *is a chain-forming diatom. The spiral form of the chain aids the diatom's buoyancy—important because diatoms have no means of locomotion but require light and therefore surface contact for photosynthesis. Diatoms also improve their buoyancy by storing the products of photosynthesis as oil, which is lighter than water.*
Narragansett Bay, Rhode Island. Paul Hargraves.

overleaf: *Herring gulls. Appledore Island, Maine. Thomas Wiewandt.*

MATT BIONDI

Olympic Gold Medalist Swimmer and Co-Founder of the Delphys Foundation

I haven't spent a great deal of time in the ocean, but I have nonetheless had some memorable experiences there. One of my most memorable was swimming with free dolphins in the Bahamas while making an educational videotape for the Delphys Foundation.

The Delphys Foundation is a small nonprofit organization based in Santa Barbara, which is involved in dolphin-oriented research and education. The film we made included footage of competitive swimmers and Atlantic spotted dolphins interacting in the clear, blue Bahamian waters.

The people we chose to put in the water as ambassadors of our kind were comfortable in the water. Among them were backstroker David Berkoff, synchronized swimmer Tracie Ruiz-Conforto, the synchronized swimming duo of Karen and Sarah Josephson, and me—all Olympic medalists. Through years of training, we have become accustomed to holding our breath for long periods of time, to free-diving easily, and to swimming smoothly.

Dolphins use echolocation to identify objects, and in the water we

Spotted dolphins. Little Bahama Bank. James D. Watt.

could really feel the echoes pulsing through our bodies as the dolphins headed toward us. They were inspecting us with those echoes, and I think they could sense that we were comfortable in the water with them.

The faster I would go to keep up with the dolphins, the faster they would go. They were always faster, always one up on me. There were a few games we could

play in the water with them. Sometimes we would go in circles, and the dolphins circled with us, always staying on the outside. If we grew tired and stopped, they continued to circle around us.

As a swimmer, I was interested in the biomechanics of dolphin movement. There were two things about the dolphins that interested me, neither of which I was really able to transfer as successfully as I would have liked to competitive swimming. The first thing was the hydrodynamic profile of a dolphin. They're so streamlined and efficient in the water. To see them give a kick and glide is pretty impressive, and since then I have often tried to imagine what it would feel like to be a dolphin and I have used that image when kicking off a pool wall. Coincidentally, the kick in the butterfly is known as the "dolphin kick." Secondly, dolphins derive most of their thrust from the upward motion of their tails, whereas humans do so from the downward movement of their feet. After watching the dolphins, I tried to get power from my upkick as well.

By holding the dolphins' interest and keeping them curious, we had many long swims with them. Some lasted up to two hours. There were days when the dolphins never came, and other days when they came around five or six times; it was their world, and they were free to come and go as they pleased. This is my most treasured memory of the dolphins. Instead of intruding on their world, we felt, at least for a while, like welcomed guests, and that's an incredible feeling.

Spotted dolphin. As one of the fastest human swimmers in the world, Matt Biondi was particularly interested in how dolphins move through the water. The dolphin's streamlined body is well suited to the marine environment, and its efficiency is heightened by the fact that a dolphin's skin is flexible enough to reconfigure itself to cut down on turbulence of water flow. A dolphin can generate enormous push with the upthrust of its tail. Dolphins swim fastest when they are "running," making a series of arcing leaps and spending as little time as possible in the water. Dolphins also increase their speed by riding the bow waves of ships. Little Bahama Bank. James D. Watt.

AL GIDDINGS

Emmy Award Winner and Underwater Director of Photography for The Deep *and* The Abyss

I had one of my most humbling experiences while making my first dives with humpback whales. I had never been in the water with a really large marine mammal, and my first inner-space encounter with these magic marine creatures was memorable.

It occurred in the 1960s, while I was working in Hawaii on a film called *Gentle Giants*. I had a wonderful moment with a huge female and her newborn calf. The mother whale allowed me to swim to within a few feet of her, so close that I could peer into her large, dark eye. In the background I could hear the sounds of other whales singing. The singers were so loud that the sound assaulted the air spaces within my body.

Staring into the mother whale's great eye left little question as to whether I was being pondered by a wonderfully intelligent animal. Her roving eye was clearly a window into a large, thinking brain. Most eyes in the undersea world are without spark and personality. Sharks have a black, expressionless eye—there is very little indication of any real emotion. It's very different with whales, especially humpbacks. You quickly become aware that they're thinking at a level closer to yours. There's great depth to a whale's eye, and that first encounter was a rare and magic moment.

Humpback whale. Alaska.
Michio Hoshino.

As I filmed the whales, I trembled, not from fear but out of a feeling of exhilaration. I knew it was the first time anyone had recorded really detailed underwater shots of humpback whales. My first film work with whales was before whale watching was in vogue. In the 1960s, people thought it was dangerous to be close to these enormous creatures. A fully mature humpback female can weigh 90,000 pounds.

I soon learned a number of special techniques that helped me approach these large and swift animals. In the early days most of my best shots were taken while free-diving. When a whale approached me from below I would hyperventilate, take a last deep breath at the surface, and slowly descend to forty or fifty feet. My heart would pound as the dark oncoming whale closed the distance. I used extreme wide-angle lenses on a small 16mm camera to avoid making any mechanical sounds. A breath-hold dive without scuba is more dolphin-like, and the whales tolerate your presence without being frightened.

In my first years of undersea filming, the most exciting animals I encountered were sharks, and the most stimulating of all the sharks, of course, was the great white. However, none of my shark experiences proved to be as humbling and provocative as my first encounter with great whales. Who would believe that watching a whale could make one's blood rush more than swimming with a great white shark? Most people think sharks are the most exciting animals in the sea, but whales affect me more. Being a few feet from a forty-ton mother and her calf, in the open ocean, while a chorus of escort whales filled the sea with their flutelike sounds, was truly overwhelming.

Humpback whale and calf. In more than two decades of under-
water filming and photography, Al Giddings rates his most
exciting times as those spent diving with humpback whales and
listening to their songs.
Doug Perrine.

Chapter Two
THE ENERGY OF LIFE

Life thrives on energy. The flow of energy through most ecosystems begins with sunlight, which is converted by photosynthetic plants into the chemical energy of life—living tissue. Chemical energy is transferred then from one organism to another within an ecosystem, and at each step some of the energy is released as heat.

A plant or animal uses energy for motion, growth, maintaining health, and reproduction. Some energy is expelled as waste. When an organism is eaten by another organism, its energy is transferred. Each passing of energy from one organism to another is part of a food chain. Just as prairie grass— nurtured by the sun, water, and minerals—feeds the buffalo, which is eaten by the wolf, so, too, does ocean kelp feed the sea urchin, which is eaten by the starfish.

Food chains interconnect in networks called "food webs." In the ocean, the most complex food webs involving large numbers of species are found in nutrient-poor tropical and open ocean waters, while the nutrient-rich coastal and polar environments tend to have simpler food webs defined by fewer species. When food is scarce, it is more difficult for one species to become strong enough to overpower the competition. In contrast, in areas where food is abundant, those species that can reproduce or grow the fastest consume the food rapidly, outstripping other species and driving them out.

In marine environments, energy moves into and out of ecosystems. Energy escapes through heat loss, the sinking of waste materials and dead bodies, the dispersal of reproductive life stages, and with migrating adults. Equally, all these losses are gains for other ecosystems; life in the ocean is interconnected.

Waves are created by winds, tides, and undersea disturbances.
Waves contain enormous kinetic energy, and when they break, the
impact force can be several tons per square foot.
Rye, New Hampshire. Michael Baytoff.

LIGHT AND PHOTOSYNTHESIS
IN THE OCEAN

On land, and in the ocean, photosynthesis—the use of solar energy to convert carbon dioxide and water into the biochemical energy of plant life—is the foundation of the web of life. However, sunlight penetrates ocean waters poorly, and this has a profound effect on the nature of ocean life and, ultimately, on the ecology of the planet.

Some of the sunlight that strikes the ocean is immediately reflected back into the air. The *intensity* of the remaining light that penetrates below the surface of the water diminishes sharply with depth, because it is absorbed or scattered by water molecules and by whatever is dissolved or suspended in the water. Even in the clearest water, 60 percent of sunlight is absorbed within a few feet of the surface, and less than 1 percent of the light reaches down to a depth of 300 feet.

Different colors of light penetrate water differently, and this affects the distribution of species that depend upon sunlight. The way ocean waters transmit light of different wavelengths depends partly upon the nature of water itself and partly upon what is dissolved in the water.

Sunlight or white light consists of a spectrum of colors, ranging from blue at the shorter visible wavelengths, through green and yellow, to red at longer visible wavelengths. In the atmosphere, the red end of the spectrum penetrates more than the blue. In seawater, the pattern is reversed: the shorter wavelengths of blue light penetrate deepest and the longer wavelengths of red light are rapidly absorbed. Even in the clearest ocean waters 99 percent of red light is absorbed in the top 15 to 30 feet. Thus, the clearest open-ocean waters usually appear blue, for these waters are most transparent to blue light. Murky coastal waters, on the other hand, tend to

Australian sea lion. Seals and sea lions are sleekly shaped for maximum speed when chasing fishes and squid.
Australia. Marty Snyderman.

above: *Coral reef table. Reefs are densely packed habitats, and coral colonies, each composed of innumerable tiny coral polyps, battle furiously with each other for space. Some corals expand their bodies to engulf and digest rival corals. To ward off such attacks, some corals grow tentacles with stinging organelles. Philippines. Carl Roessler.*

left: *Coral polyps. Although coral polyps are animals, they require sunlight to grow. Corals are hosts to zooxanthellae, a species of microalgae that through photosynthesis provides nourishment and oxygen to the coral; in turn, the coral provide nutrients and protection to the zooxanthellae. The symbiosis is vital; corals with zooxanthellae grow 90 percent faster than those without. Red Sea. Amos Nachoum.*

overleaf: *Giant clam and soft coral. Giant clams live in shallow water and open their shells toward the surface in order to expose the microscopic algae living in their tissue to sunlight. The bright blue-green mantle houses the photosynthetic cells. Great Barrier Reef, Australia. Fred Bavendam.*

appear green, for green light typically penetrates deepest there.

The transmission of light in water determines the vertical extent of the so-called euphotic zone—the volume of surface water where light can support photosynthesis. Species that photosynthesize exhibit a variety of forms and pigmentation, to keep themselves within reach of the sun's rays, and to enable them to most effectively use the sun's energy.

Wherever the bottom of the sea lies within the euphotic zone, large seaweeds will flourish. Giant kelp are able to anchor to the bottom at depths where light intensity is very low, because their buoyant fronds float at the surface, attached by stalks up to 300 feet long. Seaweeds are found in only one open-ocean area: in the Sargasso Sea near Bermuda a species of brown seaweed known as sargassum clumps into free-floating rafts that

harbor their own mini-communities of specially adapted animals.

Most photosynthesizers that float in open waters, however, are minute: microscopic single cells or aggregates of several cells have developed means of flotation enabling them to stay near the ocean surface, and thus near light. Many species of these microalgae, or phytoplankton, have developed elaborate shapes that increase their surface-to-volume ratio, giving them the benefit of maximum lift in turbulent waters. They may also produce oil within their cells to increase their buoyancy. Some microalgae are mobile by virtue of flagella—whip-like filaments that propel them small distances through the water.

Kelp forest. Giant kelp plants live in ocean waters that are less transparent to the light wavelengths most useful for photosynthesis. To maximize use of the available light, kelp have extra light-absorbing pigments that work in conjunction with chlorophyll to make the process of photosynthesis more efficient. Their fronds are wrinkled to increase light-catching surface area and have gas-filled bulbs to float the fronds near the sunlit surface water. California. Howard Hall.

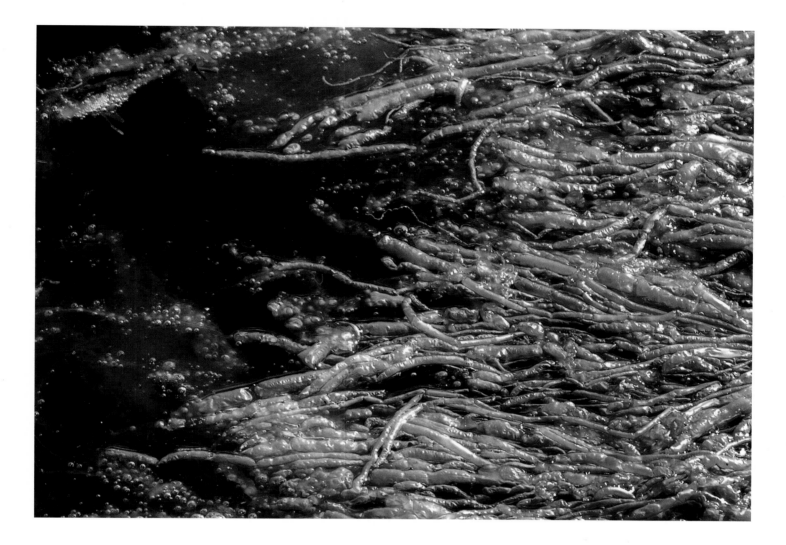

Sunlight is rendered useful to living organisms chiefly through the activity of plant pigments, chemical substances that act as catalysts for photosynthesis. The most vital of these is chlorophyll. While all marine plants employ chlorophyll, many have adapted other pigments to help capture the limited light available in the ocean. Hence, pigments may tint a seaweed green, brown, golden brown, yellow-green, red, purple, or blue-green. Accordingly, seaweeds are categorized into three major groups defined by their predominant pigmentation: green, brown, and red. Several other groups include only microalgae.

Green seaweeds often grow most successfully in shallow waters, where they are exposed to red light. Many green seaweeds are intertidal and are out of the water for a short time each day. Brown algae, often known as kelp, contain carotenoids—the yellowish pigments—as well as chlorophyll. They are found both in intertidal areas and in deep coastal waters, where they can use the green light that penetrates deepest. Red algae contain red and blue pigments (biliproteins), in addition to chlorophyll.

Green hollow seaweed. There are three main groups of seaweed: red, green, and brown. Green seaweed pigments are predominantly chlorophyll pigments, and green seaweeds are therefore best able to live high in the intertidal zone, where they are frequently exposed to the greatest amount of sunlight. Green algae are the ancestors of land plants.
Appledore Island, Maine. Thomas Wiewandt.

This enhances their ability to use the yellow-green-blue portion of the light spectrum, and extends the depths to which they can grow. Similarly, several different groups of microalgae that make up phytoplankton have sets of pigments that enhance the absorption of light for photosynthesis.

above: *The red mangrove is one of the few flowering plants found in salt water. Land plants have difficulty adapting to the marine environment; in order to absorb water and nutrients, their roots must sink into water-saturated soil. The prop roots of mangroves are partly above the waterline and help aerate the waterlogged roots that extend into the mud.*
Key Biscayne, Florida. Doug Perrine.

left: *Great blue heron. These birds are found in mangrove swamps, inland lakes, on sea grass beds, and in other fresh and saltwater wetland habitats.*
Everglades National Park, Florida. Frank Balthis.

PRIMARY PRODUCTION
AND GRAZING

In a living plant cell, the sun's energy is captured by chlorophyll and transferred to chemical bonds holding together energy-rich sugar molecules, which the plant fabricates from carbon dioxide and water. The transforming process continues in the cell as various molecules are built from the products of photosynthesis, and a number of minerals are absorbed from the environment: nitrogen, phosphorus, sulfur, magnesium, calcium, iron, and others. Here is the production line for creating the essential structural building blocks of the living organism, the fuel for future energy requirements, and the DNA for reproduction. Here is the site of the continual chemical transformations that are the life process.

The production of organic material from inorganic matter is called primary production. In most of the sunlit areas of the sea, the primary producers are the microalgae that drift in surface waters. Along the fringes of the ocean, larger plants such as seaweeds are the primary producers.

Plants in the sea have the same basic needs as those on the land: water, nutrition, and light. For marine plants, of course, water is no problem. And since seawater is a solution of minerals in which certain essential nutrients may be limited, plant populations may increase or decrease as nutrients become more or less plentiful. The real challenge for marine plants, however, is to maximize their exposure to light. Consequently, microalgae have evolved a variety of shapes that allow them to stay afloat near the surface of the ocean, where the sunlight is greatest. The elaborate chains, spirals, projections, and

Queen triggerfish. Triggerfish often graze on algae on coral reefs. Their powerful mouths are also ideally formed for devouring the corals upon which they feed. The bones of the upper jaw join together to form a beak, and the mouth contains three rows of teeth, which the triggerfish grinds together to mulch food. Lighthouse Reef, Belize. Doug Perrine.

Sea squirts are filter feeders and live on small plankton and fine detritus. They pull food-laden water through their siphonlike gut, filter out particles, and squirt it back out; hence their name. British Virgin Islands. Al Grotell.

fins that help increase their flotation also make them very beautiful when viewed under a microscope.

Where there is grass there are grazers, so the waters where light supports photosynthesis abound with herbivorous animals that eat sea plants. Marine herbivores range from planktonic animals such as protozoa, larvae, crustaceans, and jellyfish, which feed on planktonic microalgae, to sea urchins, marine snails, and fish, which graze on seaweeds, to manatees, which munch on submerged sea grasses.

Grazing on seaweeds is a simple matter of wandering over a bed of algae and biting and munching on the plant material. Fish and shellfish either nibble around the edges of the plants or scrape the young sprouts off the rocks. Grazing on minute phytoplankton (plant plankton), however, is a different story altogether.

Since phytoplankton drift in the sunlit waters of the oceans, animals that want to eat them must do the same, or else they must be able to swim into those waters at will. Tiny crustaceans often make long daily excursions up and down the water col-

umn, so at least part of each day is spent in the phy-toplankton zone. Jellyfish and ctenophores, which look something like jellyfish, drift on ocean currents, but they can move a little bit on their own, and this movement is generally directed upward.

The soup of microalgae floating near the sur-face presents a special kind of challenge to would-be herbivores. Catching and eating microalgae one by one is a very inefficient method for all but the single-celled protozoa. Larger plankton-eating animals have developed feeding mechanisms that act like a fisherman's net: they strain their food out of the water. It is the preferred method for harvesting small phytoplankton and zooplankton (animal plankton).

Virtually every major taxonomic group of animals in the sea includes some species that are fil-ter feeders. Although the specifics of the mechanism

Marine iguana feeding on algae. Found in the Galápagos Islands off Ecuador, the marine iguana is the only oceangoing lizard. It is cold-blooded, and to survive in cold waters, the marine iguana first lies on shore on sunny rocks until it has warmed up; it then dives into the water and feeds at depths of up to 30 feet. Marine iguanas have sharp teeth for prying algae off rocks. Despite their fierce looks, they are shy and inoffensive.
Galápagos. Carl Roessler.

Moon jelly. A suspension feeder, the moon jelly drifts through the ocean catching plankton on the sticky surface of the bell. Rows of cilia then move the food to the mouth, underneath the bell. The moon jelly also swims, alternately contracting and relaxing the bell edges to push away the water behind it.
Atlantic Ocean off Rhode Island. Eric Schwarz.

vary from species to species, the goal is the same: to remove enough microalgae or tiny animals from the water to provide a steady food supply. Again and again, animals in different lines of evolution have independently arrived at basically the same solution.

Sponges, sea squirts, and most bivalve shell-fish (mollusks) are filter feeders, as are a few marine snails and numerous crustaceans. Larvae are usually filter feeders as well. Several species of fish and a whole class of whales are also filter feeders.

The mechanism of filter feeding involves a range of structural adaptations. The larvae of most invertebrates are filter feeders. Many are of the sort sometimes referred to as "whirlers." They have rows of tiny hairlike structures, called cilia, that create water currents, and these cause the larva to spin. As water flows past the body, particles are caught up by the cilia, embedded in mucus, and carried along channels to the mouth.

Sometimes the adaptations are associated with the outer skin, as in jellyfish; sometimes with gills, as in polychaete worms; sometimes with

siphons or tubes, as in a few marine snails and in almost all sea squirts. The particles trapped by simple adhesion or by filtering will include living cells as well as nonliving particles of debris. All are ingested, often right along with the mucus.

Crustaceans belong to the division of animals called Arthropoda, a division that includes insects, spiders, and centipedes. As insects swarm on land, crustaceans—characterized by five pairs of jointed legs—swarm in the sea. They include the small insectlike forms such as copepods; the larger and more familiar shrimplike forms, including krill and true shrimp; and barnacles; and they are all filter feeders. As larvae, crabs and lobsters take full advantage of the microalgal broth at the surface; as adults, they feast instead on the detritus on the seafloor.

Whale shark. Up to 50 feet long and 40,000 pounds in weight, the whale shark is the largest fish in the world. A filter feeder, it subsists on tiny shrimplike krill and other plankton, and small fish. The whale shark feeds by opening its mouth and passing an enormous quantity of water through the mouth and gills, trapping prey on its gill rakers. The shark then closes its mouth, expells the water, and swallows the food. The amount of water passed through a whale shark's mouth is about 2,000 tons per hour. Hawaii. James D. Watt.

overleaf: *Sea urchin. Caribbean. Scott Frier.*

Crustacean filter feeders have evolved special appendages that are covered with stiff feathery hair and that work independently or together to move water and form a netlike filter that traps particles of a specific size range. Barnacles feed by means of a rhythmic extension and withdrawal of pairs of jointed appendages with long, thin projections, which work together to form a sweeping net. In krill, forelegs are adapted to move the animal forward and the water backward into a basketlike structure, formed by intermeshed appendages, designed to trap most microalgae. Krill are in turn eaten by baleen whales, which are the largest filter feeders in the ocean.

above left: *Feather duster worms. The feathery plumes are the worms' respiratory and food-collecting systems. The feathers are extended for filter feeding and absorption of oxygen, and are just a part of the worms that live in tubes burrowed into the coral reef. Bahamas. James Gritz.*

top right: *Coral polyps open for feeding. Corals filter tiny plankton from the water, and densely packed corals such as these will compete fiercely for food. Bahamas. James Gritz.*

bottom right: *Gorgonian polyps. Gorgonians are related to corals, jellyfish, and anemones. All have in common the use of tentacles and stinging cells for defense or to stun prey. Solomon Islands. Burt Jones & Maurine Shimlock.*

opposite: *The crinoid feather star is a filter feeder and can furl and unfurl its arms at will. The mouth lies at the base of the arms and faces upward. The feathered arms collect planktonic food and then deliver it to the mouth via grooves running down each arm. South Pacific. Howard Hall.*

PREDATORS AND DETRITIVORES

Marine predators use a wide variety of techniques to catch their meals. Some actively search for their prey, others wait for it to come to them, still others lure their prey in. Some predators, such as certain species of jellyfish and sea anemones, are not able to pursue their meals, so they trap and immobilize their prey by injecting tiny stinging cells called nematocysts. Then they slowly ingest the victim, which is typically a small fish or soft invertebrate, although even shelled animals can be trapped by these predators.

A surprising number of much more mobile animals lie in wait for unsuspecting prey. The stargazer, a remorseful-looking fish whose eyes and mouth are situated on the top of its large head, wiggles into the soft sediments, striking only when the victim is directly overhead. Using a similar tactic, moray eels hide in dark crevasses in coral or rock until some tempting fish or octopus swims close. The many-toothed eel then darts out and snatches it.

More direct stalking of prey is, of course, common. Starfish simply crawl right up to or on their prey, wrap an arm or several arms around it, pry open a shell (if the prey is a bivalve), and devour the contents. Starfish are effective predators of sea urchins, mussels, clams, coral, and many other generally sedentary invertebrates. One of the most voracious predators in the sea is the crown-of-thorns starfish, which feeds on coral. It has been credited with wiping out vast areas of coral reefs in Australia and elsewhere in the Pacific. Starfish are common inhabitants of rocky seashores and soft sediments, but they are also found on abyssal sediments and on the walls of the deepest trenches.

Tiger shark. Of 300-odd species of sharks, only 25 to 40 are considered dangerous to humans, and the tiger shark is one of those. The tiger shark primarily eats fish, squid, crabs, and lobsters, but it will occasionally attack people. The tiger shark grows up to 20 feet long and gives birth to live young. Bahama Banks. James D. Watt.

Fish that move over long distances to find food or to migrate to breeding grounds have evolved a variety of streamlined shapes to increase their swimming speed and efficiency. Almost all fish are cold-blooded—that is, their body temperature is the same as the surrounding water. But tuna and some species of sharks, including the fastest-swimming species, are warm-blooded. Their intense, vigorous motion is linked with their ability to regulate body temperature.

The largest predators of the sea are sharks and whales. Sharks are primitive fish found at all depths of coastal and open-ocean waters. Whales are air-breathing mammals that require frequent contact with the surface, but they are able to dive down to great depths. There are species among both sharks and whales that feed on large prey, as well as species—the largest sharks and whales, in fact—that filter-feed on small planktonic animals.

There are about 300 species of sharks. Their behavior varies widely. Some are slow and restful, others are in constant motion; some are docile, others fierce. All have teeth, but only twenty-five to

above: *Crown-of-thorns starfish eating coral. The crown-of-thorns is a voracious predator on reef-building corals, and has decimated numerous reefs in the South Pacific. It can travel rapidly, rolling in the waves like a tumbleweed. The crown-of-thorns feeds by extending its stomach out of its body and over its prey, to secrete digestive juices over the victim. Thailand. Doug Perrine.*

right: *Sea otters are keystone predators in maintaining the ecological balance of giant kelp forests; they eat and hold in check the sea urchins that otherwise would eat all the kelp. Sea otters also eat abalone, other shellfish, and fish. Sea otters have no blubber but are insulated instead by fur, which traps a layer of warm air next to their skin. To generate enough energy for warmth in cold waters, they must consume the equivalent of a quarter of their body weight every day. They rarely come ashore. Monterey Bay, California. F. Stuart Westmorland.*

left: *Leopard moray. Morays can quickly dart in and out of the holes and crevasses in which they like to hide.*
Kona, Hawaii. Kevin & Cat Sweeney.

below: *Moray eel in orange coral. A continuously opening and closing mouth filled with sharp teeth gives the moray eel a fierce appearance. Like almost any animal, a moray will strike if cornered and provoked. However, morays are simply breathing when they move their jaws, and are shy, rather than aggressive. Divers sometimes make friends with morays, feeding them bits of food and often, as with dogs, petting them on the head.*
Izu Peninsula, Japan. David Doubilet.

The sperm whale is the largest of the toothed whales (60 feet) and is an avid hunter powerful enough to swallow a large shark in a single gulp. Some scientists have estimated that sperm whales can dive as deep as 10,500 feet. Whereas humpback whales sing in tones, sperm whales click in patterns that resemble a type of Morse code. The sperm whale has the largest brain of any animal. Hawaii. Flip Nicklin.

forty species are considered dangerous to human swimmers. Sharks are found in all oceans, from warm, shallow waters to colder, deeper waters. Some species are restricted to the deepest ocean. Rays, close relatives of the sharks, are also predators, and eat small invertebrates or filter plankton.

Toothed whales often feed on schools of fish, gobbling them one or many at a time, depending upon the whale's size relative to the fish. They may also seek out large, solitary animals. The sperm whale, for example, is a noted predator upon the giant squid—a delicacy that may weigh as much as a few hundred pounds.

There are several species of baleen whales, all of which are filter feeders and all of which are extremely large. The word *baleen* refers to the comb-like plate that strains zooplankton from huge volumes of water. Various species use the baleen in different ways. The right whale skims the surface collecting food in its long baleen plates. The humpback gulps down huge mouthfuls of water, raising its tongue to force water through shorter baleen plates. The gray whale plows the bottom sediments, forcing water, mud, and gravel through its baleen plate, trapping small animals that live in the sediment.

Some of the most ferocious-looking predators are found among the mid- to deep-water fishes. Their underslung scowls or beaks are often lined with needle-sharp teeth, and their bodies often bear strange patterns of light-producing organs. These fish could be monsters out of a horror tale, except that they are small, a few inches long at most.

below: *Barracuda. Found around coral reefs and common in most tropical waters, barracuda prey on small fish such as silversides and mackerel. Up to 6 feet in length, and armed with wicked-looking teeth, barracuda are often greatly feared by humans. In fact, unprovoked attacks are rare.*
Solomon Islands. Marty Snyderman.

right: *Pacific giant octopus eating a turbot. The octopus uses its tentacles to grab prey, then bites the victim with its beak. An octopus can also inject a paralyzing poison into its prey.*
Barkley Sound, B.C., Canada. Fred Bavendam.

overleaf: *Hammerhead sharks. Sea of Cortez. Marty Snyderman.*

Beneath the open-ocean surface lie 10,000 to 20,000 feet of coursing ocean water where light dims until it is finally extinguished altogether. As the relatively shallow euphotic zone in which photosynthesis can occur gives way to the vast volume of twilit and darkened waters below, grazers moving freely between the upper and lower worlds join sinking organic detritus—dead cells and fecal pellets—to form the lifeline linking the primary production of the surface waters with the food web of the deep. This web consists exclusively of predators and detritivores, or consumers of detritus.

Most organic detritus carries associated bacteria and yeasts and is a rich food source. The plankton of deep ocean waters, which include many filter feeders, feed primarily on particulate detritus and tiny animals. Other detritivores on or near the seafloor search for large chunks of detritus upon which to scavenge. If they're lucky, they find dead whales. Crabs, starfish, and the like will converge in a feeding frenzy upon a newly-settled mass. Such temporary feasts allow a diverse, albeit transient, community to survive in the otherwise uneventful bottom sediments.

above: *Moustache conger eel with yellow tang. Rather than pursuing their prey, eels usually lie in wait. The yellow tang could easily outswim the conger eel, but fell victim to the eel's ambush. Maui, Hawaii. Steve Rosenberg.*

left: *Humpback whales feeding. Humpbacks are filter feeders and eat large plankton such as krill, and small fish and squid. They often follow a practice called "bubble netting" in which they form a ring of air bubbles that tends to drive prey into concentrations. The humpbacks have pleated throats that expand to allow them to swallow a ton of water in a gulp. They use their tongues to push water through the baleen plates, which are comblike and bristly on the inside, in order to trap krill and other food. Seabirds feed on the sea life the humpbacks force to the surface. North Atlantic Ocean. Michael Baytoff.*

REPRODUCTION AND DISPERSAL

REPRODUCTION AND DISPERSAL

The ocean is the source and cradle of life; it is where all the major divisions of life are to be found in a profusion of biological diversity and in all imaginable varieties of reproductive strategies. In the moving, nurturing, fluid environment of the sea, dispersal is an important condition of procreation. The energy of ocean currents indirectly contributes to the growth of living organisms and the perpetuation of species. It supports the early stages of animals with rich blooms of food organisms and it carries them to new settling grounds.

Reproductive strategies range from the very simple to the very complex, depending in part on the scale of the organism and in part upon the evolutionary history of the species. At the smallest end of the scale, a single cell divides and becomes two individuals. This simple cell division is fundamental to reproduction in microalgae. Larger and more complex plants and even a few animals may also increase their populations simply by creating two or more individuals from one; that is, by asexual reproduction. Some "bud" off exact copies of themselves. In this manner, sea squirts form colonies, usually with their own characteristic shapes. A bump of tissue forms on the side of a sea squirt body and ultimately develops into a complete new sea squirt, adding to the colony of separate but associated individuals. Other organisms—seaweeds, for instance—release asexual spores. In others, fragments of tissue break off. The spores and tissue fragments develop into new individuals identical to the parent.

More commonly, marine animals reproduce sexually. Sexual reproduction is general among both plants and animals. It involves the fusion of two

Narwhals. The narwhal's tusk was once passed off by traders as the mythical unicorn's horn. The tusk's function is uncertain, but it may be used as a weapon in mating battles or as a tool for breaking through ice. The tusk can grow up to 8 feet long and is actually the male narwhal's left tooth; in rare cases the right tooth will also develop into a tusk. Females do not develop tusks. Canada. Flip Nicklin.

~ 95 ~

gametes, egg and sperm, usually from two parents, so that the offspring are a genetic mixture.

In the nurturing soup of ocean water, it is generally not critical to early life stages—gametes, eggs, larvae, embryos—to be protected within a parent's body or for the young to be cared for by their parents. As a result, live birth is rare among marine animals; it is usual only among sharks and rays, extremely rare among all other fish, and is rarer yet among invertebrates. Marine mammals, however, entered the sea from the land, and they give birth to young that are already developed to a relatively advanced, juvenile stage.

The dispersion of offspring may begin as early as the gamete stage, with fertilization between egg and sperm occurring in the water, generally not far from the parents. This is common among seaweeds and numerous sea animals. Since successful fertilization in open water relies upon the chance encounter of a male and female gamete, spawning of eggs and sperm is very often orchestrated by environmental or chemical signals so that large numbers of

above: *Mating nudibranchs. Nudibranchs are hermaphrodites. Any two nudibranchs can mate because each has both male and female sexual characteristics. They simply link up, while facing in opposite directions as these two are, and exchange sperm. Each will bear fertilized eggs.*
Red Sea. Chris Newbert.

left: *Mating red Irish lords. Bony fish reproduce in a variety of ways. Some keep their fertilized eggs inside their body, some build nests to protect eggs, and others simply eject eggs and sperm into the water. Typically, fish lay incredible numbers of eggs, millions in some cases, on the chance that a limited few will develop into adulthood.*
Northern Vancouver Island, Canada. F. Stuart Westmorland.

overleaf: *Nudibranch eggs. Lord Howe Island, Australia. David Doubilet.*

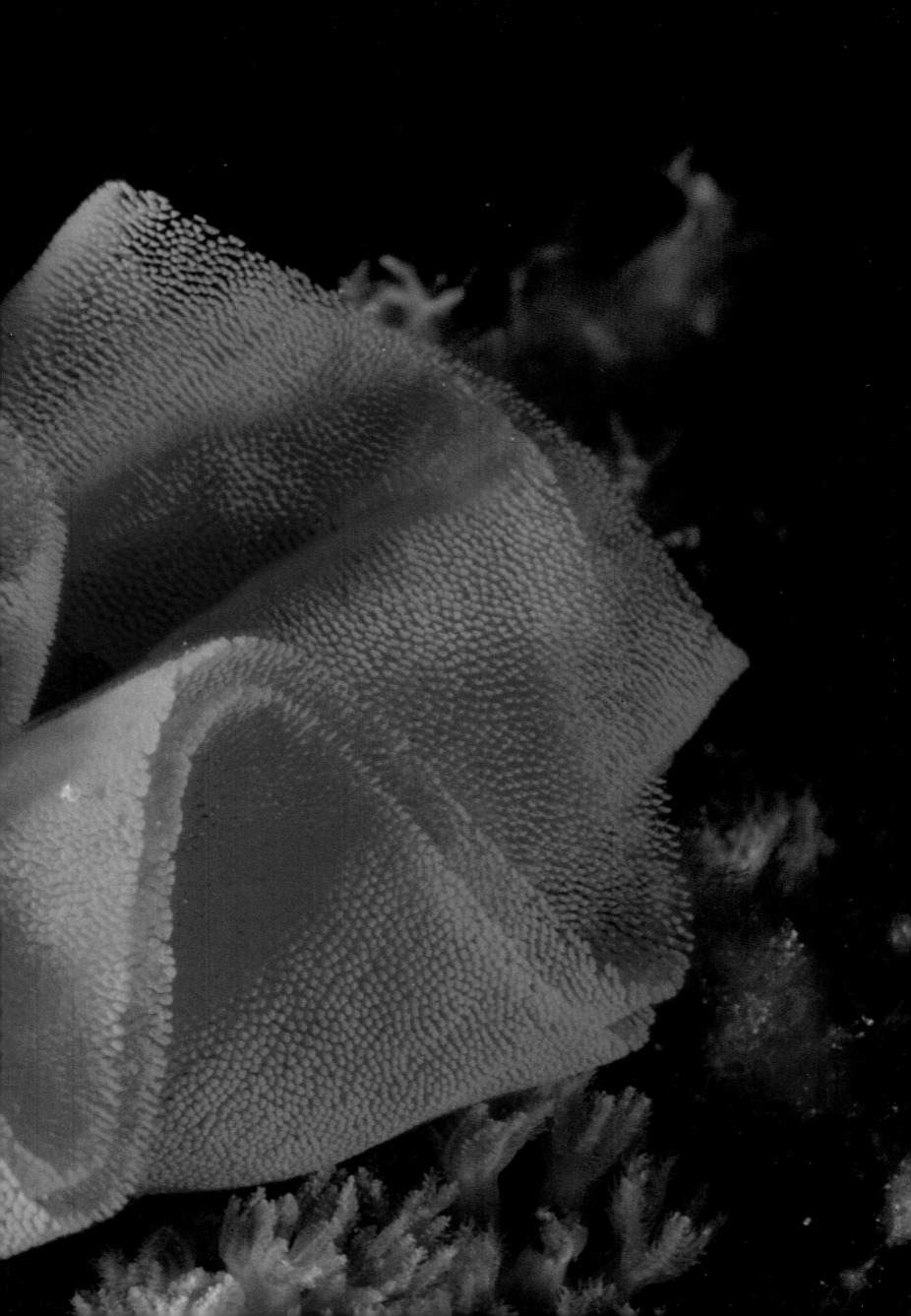

male and female gametes of the same species are released simultaneously. Abalone, for example, respond to a hormone that they themselves release into the water: once a few individual abalones release the hormone, the entire abalone community in the area will spawn, with dense masses of eggs and sperm entering the surrounding waters in unison.

Horseshoe crabs make use of both environmental and chemical signals. In spring, when the water has warmed to about 70° F, and the tide is the highest tide of the month (the full-moon tide), the female crab comes inshore to spawn at the tide's highest reach. The male follows, for he is attracted by a pheromone exuded by the female. After digging a small hole, the female deposits her mass of gray-blue eggs into it. Stimulated by another pheromone released with the eggs, the male expels his sperm over the mass. Then the adults retreat with the ebbing tide.

This mating ritual is eagerly witnessed by many potential predators, especially shorebirds. They move in, and, in a frenzy of feeding, gobble up as many of the eggs as they can before blowing sand covers them up.

A month later, at the next full-moon tide, the baby horseshoe crabs hatch out and burrow upward, where the high tide sweeps them into the sea. When they are quite small, they swim freely in the water, later settling into a more sedentary life at the bottom.

Sponge releasing a cloud of larvae by pumping water through its body cavity. Sponges are hermaphrodites, producing both sperm and eggs. The eggs usually remain inside the sponge waiting for sperm to float in and fertilize them.
Grand Bahama Island. Doug Perrine.

Dispersion for many marine animals is enhanced when the fertilized egg develops into a larva. Most larvae—those of crustaceans, mollusks, jellyfish, and starfish, for instance—do not resemble their parents. Instead, their forms are adapted for life in the surface waters, often in the microlayer, where there is a plentiful supply of microalgae for food. Planktonic fish larvae, for instance, bear little resemblance to the adult fish. They start out as tadpole-like creatures with large eyes, without colored scales, and sometimes with a large yolk sac still attached for nutrition. Like all larvae, they eventually develop into juveniles that look like small versions of the adult.

Some larvae, however, are miniatures of the adults that they will become. Octopuses and squids, for instance, produce tiny young around an eighth of an inch long. In some marine fish and invertebrates, there is no true larval stage. The horseshoe crab lays large eggs in which the embryo develops; eventually, babies closely resembling the adults are hatched out.

Though most eggs are left on their own, in some species a parent tends them until they hatch. This is true for octopus species and sea horses. The

above: The female horseshoe crab is digging the hole into which she will deposit her eggs. She will lay a few hundred eggs, which will be fertilized by a male and hatch into larvae after several months. The larvae look like miniature adults but will drift and swim near the surface until they become adults at three years of age. The eggs and young are heavily preyed upon, especially by seabirds, and adults are gathered by humans for medical research. Delaware Bay, New Jersey. Michael Baytoff.

below: Horseshoe crab eggs. Delaware Bay, New Jersey. Michael Baytoff.

octopus mother blows oxygen-rich water over the eggs and broods them for about a month, during which time she scarcely eats. At the end of this period, the larvae hatch and are carried away by the water currents. For some time they live as plankton in the surface waters, later taking up permanent residence in deeper environs. Among sea horses, the female ejects the eggs into a brood pouch in the male, where they develop into baby sea horses and are released.

Parental care of the young beyond this stage is characteristic only of animals that have evolved from land animals: sea mammals and seabirds. Some marine animals provide extra protection for developing eggs by laying them in special egg cases. Marine snails do this, and whelks lay their eggs in chains in shallow-water moorings. Skates, which are relatives of rays, also lay their eggs in special cases; each of the eggs is enveloped in a tough purselike sac that protects the embryo until it has developed into a baby skate. The sac then splits open and the baby skate swims out to start its life. Sometimes the waves toss these cases into the debris on beaches. Beachcombers call them "mermaids' purses."

When larvae are produced, they are quickly carried on ocean currents long distances from their parents. Larvae from coastal bottom-dwellers such as crabs and starfish drift in surface waters to other coastal areas, where they eventually settle, assume the shape of the adults of their species, and adopt the bottom, or benthic, life. In the surface waters of the open ocean, planktonic larvae come from all manner of life. The larvae from coastal species swim alongside larvae from oceanic species, such as tuna and flying fish, as well as alongside larvae from deep-water species such as angler fish, which normally live between 3,000 and 9,000 feet down. Only deep-ocean, bottom-dwelling animals are apparently not represented in the surface layer; these species

Male lumpfish guarding eggs. The female lumpfish leaves after laying her eggs in a spongy mass on the rocks, and the father protects them until they hatch. In many species it is the father who cares for the developing eggs. Male sea horses and pipefish incubate eggs in a kangaroo-like brood pouch.
York, Maine. Fred Bavendam.

tend to produce large eggs that hatch directly into juveniles that feed on the detritus at those great depths.

Larvae live in surface waters for periods of a month or more before developing into their juvenile form. Among coastal benthic species, the larvae generally settle to the bottom before development occurs, often in response to a chemical signal given off by the adults of the species on the bottom. The larvae are seeking their own kind, who have sent them the message that the bottom environment is suitable for habitation. In other species, the larvae seek similar cues. Without the appropriate chemical signal, such a larva will not settle and metamorphose; it will go on living a planktonic existence until it is eaten or dies.

Oyster fishermen have long known that to maintain a productive bed of oysters where new larvae will be encouraged to settle and grow, old shells must be left in the bed. As it turns out, it is not the

Male clown fish blowing water on eggs to give them oxygen and clear away debris. A male clown fish will defend the eggs to the point of confronting and attacking larger fish; however, the parent leaves soon after the eggs are hatched.
Fiji. Scott Frier.

shells themselves that send the signal to the larvae to "make your homestead here." Rather, a species of bacteria living in association with the oysters releases the chemical signal. Similarly, abalone larvae will settle only where a certain red alga lives, and it is the alga that gives off the chemical signal. The arrangement appears to be advantageous to both species. Since abalone graze on algae, the signal indicates rich feeding grounds. At the same time, the red alga species, which is a low-growing form that encrusts rocks (and, incidentally, abalone shells), benefits from the grazing, which keeps down the competition. Taller species of algae that would shade out the little red alga are preferentially chosen by the abalone.

left: *Swell shark embryo in egg case. The embryo and yolk sac are clearly visible in the egg case. The yolk shrinks as the shark grows. Egg cases are usually laid by bottom-dwelling sharks and skates. Izu Peninsula, Japan. David Doubilet.*

below: *Swell shark emerging from egg case. Most sharks give birth to live young that have been nourished in the womb through a placenta. Others lay eggs, either inside their bodies, or in external egg cases, as the swell shark does. Shark reproduction is often a rough business. Cannibalism in the womb is common, which cuts the birth rate drastically. California. Mark Conlin.*

overleaf: *Pacific giant octopus eggs hours before hatching. Victoria, British Columbia. Fred Bavendam.*

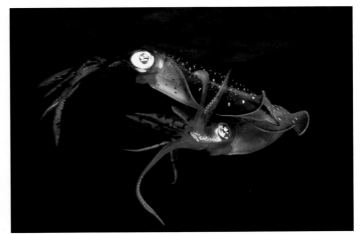

Reproduction through the dispersal of larvae and eggs has two important consequences. First, species are rarely isolated in one small habitat, as often happens on land; instead, marine species are broadly distributed. Second, the early life stages of an animal may be lived far away from its parents, perhaps in entirely different ecosystems—a dramatic difference from most land animals, which are directly cared for by their parents or at least share a habitat with them. This dispersal allows the species to flourish over a wider area, but it also means that these species' survival depends upon favorable conditions in more than one ecosystem.

This sequence shows squid mating and is perhaps the only time Caribbean reef squid have been photographed mating in their habitat. In the first three pictures above, the squid are dancing in the early stages of their mating ritual. The fourth photo is of squid eggs, which attach themselves to the ocean bottom. At right, the squid on the top turns white at the culmination of the mating dance and inserts a tentacle into the other squid. Caribbean. Scott Frier.

overleaf: *Rays. California. Howard Hall.*

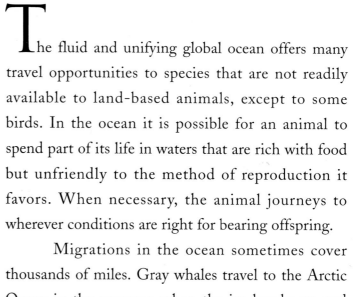

MIGRATION

The fluid and unifying global ocean offers many travel opportunities to species that are not readily available to land-based animals, except to some birds. In the ocean it is possible for an animal to spend part of its life in waters that are rich with food but unfriendly to the method of reproduction it favors. When necessary, the animal journeys to wherever conditions are right for bearing offspring.

Migrations in the ocean sometimes cover thousands of miles. Gray whales travel to the Arctic Ocean in the summer, when the ice breaks up and marine productivity soars, to take advantage of the extremely rich feeding grounds. Dense blooms of algae fuel the explosion of growth in all manner of short-lived or winter-dormant animal populations, from the ocean surface down into the bottom sediments. Gray whales feed constantly during the summer, scooping and filtering the rich stew of sediments for the many small animals harbored there. Indeed, they eat enough to sustain them for the entire year; when they move southward to the winter calving grounds of Baja California, they scarcely eat.

Salmon and herring start out life in rivers and streams. Once they begin to mature, they leave, drifting and swimming downriver and out to sea. There they spend several years living in schools and feeding on the plentiful supply of smaller oceanic animals. Finally, they return to the rivers to spawn and die.

The salmon migrations that occur each fall are particularly impressive, for these fish undertake a long, grueling journey upstream against fast-flowing

Humpback whale and calf. Humpback whales are migratory: they typically spend the summer feeding in polar regions and in winter move to warm waters near the equator, where they breed and give birth. Females give birth to single calves after a gestation period of about one year. Humpback calves, which weigh 1 ton at birth, are weaned after twelve months. Humpback whales can grow to a length of 55 feet and a weight of 65 tons and live to the age of ninety-five.
Hawaii. Flip Nicklin.

currents, dangerous rapids, and even waterfalls. Salmon are remarkable in their uncanny ability to find the exact river or stream where they were born and in their inexhaustible drive to reach the shallow stream heads where they deposit and fertilize their eggs and then, starved and exhausted, die. Completing and renewing the cycle, the corpses of the adults provide a ready food source for the young hatchlings before they themselves begin their long voyage to the sea.

Less dramatic fish migrations are common between offshore waters and estuaries, which serve as nursery areas and may offer good feeding in the spring and summer. Striped bass spawn and develop in rivers and estuaries, but they eventually move to sea, where they usually range parallel to the coast in search of food. Flounder and sole typically spawn in upper estuarine waters in the winter or early spring; in the summer they move to the mouth of the estuary or offshore. Bluefish are voracious predators,

Eye of southern right whale. Right whales earned their name because they were considered the "right" whales to hunt: despite weighing up to 50 tons, right whales float when killed, making the hunter's task much easier. Right whales are nearly extinct. Protected since the 1920s, they have not recovered from earlier slaughtering, and less than 500 are left in the Atlantic and Pacific. Patagonia, Argentina. Marty Snyderman.

feeding on small fish in coastal and estuarine waters. They move northward and southward and in and out of estuaries in coordination with periods of phytoplankton blooming.

Some seabirds have migration patterns closely keyed to events in coastal waters. For example, sanderlings and plovers winter in South America and fly northward to the Arctic to breed in the summer. They must settle in just as the Arctic insect population explodes, thus providing the young birds with a plentiful food supply. Along the long migratory journey route they depend upon estuarine food supplies to fuel their high-energy requirements. One of their annual stopovers is Delaware Bay, where they rely upon the annual release of horseshoe crab eggs. The crabs move into the bay and lay their eggs at the same time each year, and the migrating birds arrive at about the same time to feed.

Orcas vary in their patterns of movement. Those that live near Vancouver Island, for instance, are divided into groups of resident pods, which tend to live in certain areas and eat fish, and transient pods, which range up and down the coasts and feed more upon marine mammals. A few years ago a third group of orcas was discovered, with an entirely different language from the other groups. When jumping, an orca has to move at about 22 mph in order to break clear of the water. Orcas and many other marine mammals often jump when breathing in order to maintain speed, because exposing only the blowhole creates turbulence and drag and slows the animal down.
San Juan Islands, Washington. F. Stuart Westmorland.

overleaf: *Green sea turtle. Kona, Hawaii. Doug Perrine.*

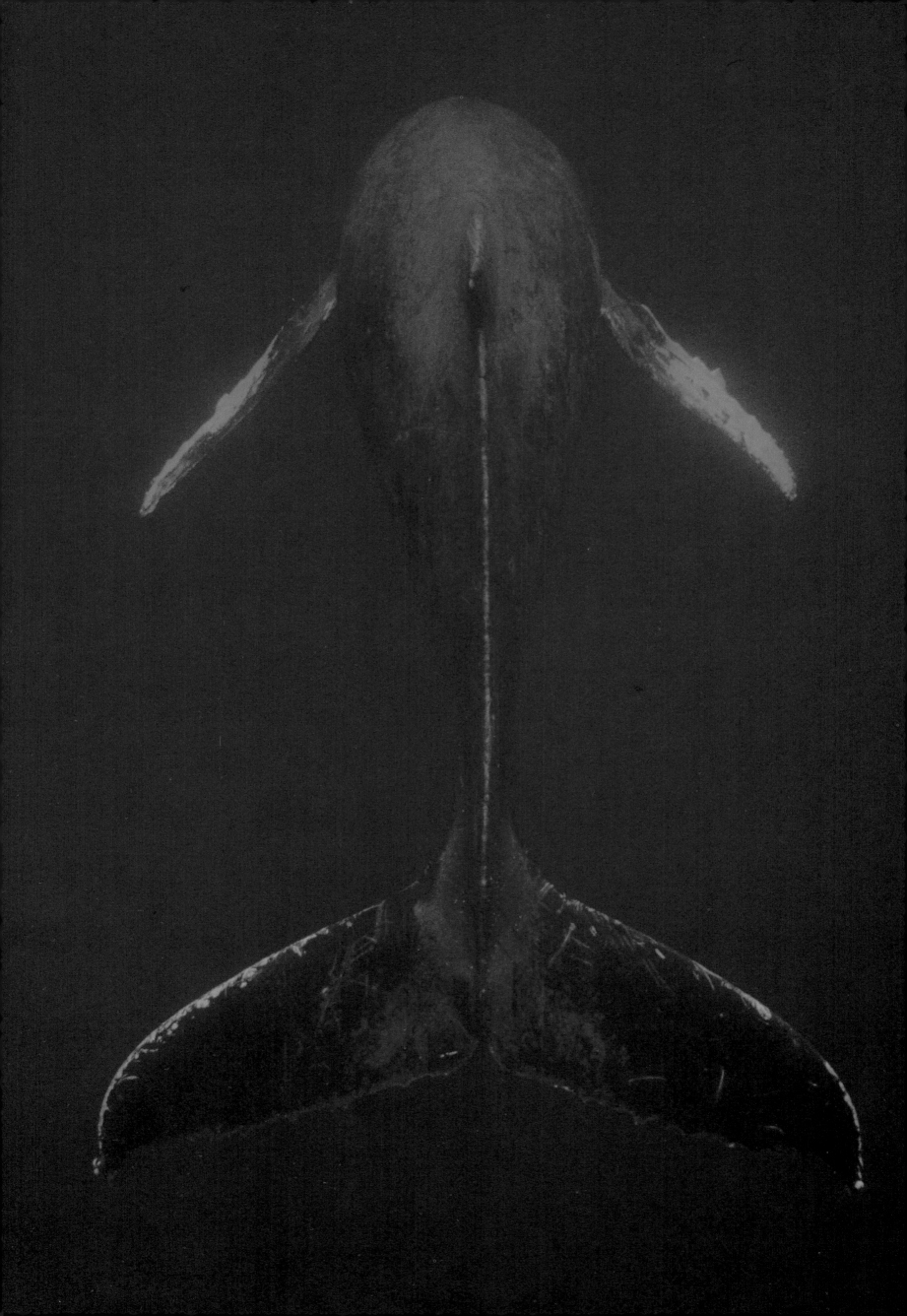

Such an intricate coordination between species with entirely different agendas could be catastrophically affected by changes in the conditions that drive the schedule. For example, if a change in global climate were to cause these various events to move out of phase, the birds might arrive at their usual destination only to find that the food they needed for survival was in short supply, or even nowhere to be found.

Whether scheduling migration, coordinating reproduction, sending out larvae to seek new environs, or searching for food, species in the ocean are dependent upon each other and upon the ocean currents. All individuals, species, and ecosystems are linked by the flow of life-sustaining energy through the ocean environment, and affected by ruptures or disturbances to those links.

above: *The ocean sunfish, or mola mola, often makes lengthy vertical migrations; on sunny days it will rest and feed on the surface, yet it also feeds on deep-sea fish. This giant grows as long as 13 feet and can weigh more than 2,000 pounds. It has few if any predators—including man, because it has little commercial value. California. Richard Herrmann.*

left: *Humpback whales communicate with each other using a complex and versatile language, which has come to be known as the song of the humpback whales. Most singing is in relatively shallow water, but the low-frequency sounds may be audible over hundreds of miles across the deep-ocean sound channel. Hawaii. Flip Nicklin.*

overleaf: *Spawning sockeye salmon. Shuswap Lake, British Columbia. F. Stuart Westmorland.*

DAVID DOUBILET

Author and Photographer of Light in the Sea *and* Pacific: An Undersea Journey

I pursue light. I really love the way light works on everything, not just in the sea but also, for example, the way gray light falls on the boundary between the sea and the land. I'm constantly looking at light.

The interesting thing about underwater photography is that natural light plays an important part in making it work, but, in addition, much of everything underwater has to be lit. You have to import light, so you have to swim with this big housing that holds two, sometimes three, strobes. I would like people to believe I'm not just one of those *paparazzi* with a flash—"Here comes the stingray, give it a blast. Here's the grouper hiding in the corner, thump it with a strobe and go on to the next thing." The problem is that a lot of the frames we're making require another piece of light; they desperately cry out for it. In essence, the giant camera with two strobes should be a movable, swimmable studio.

Sunlight comes into the sea and gets slowly absorbed, creating a soft blanket of light. In the noonday sun, even in the clearest open water, the molecules of water turn in the light and pieces of light bounce off them, resulting in slanting rays that seem to go down forever. When the sun sets in the Red Sea, there's an undersea afterglow where the white sand and the blue water seem to support the light. It's more like an alpenglow than an afterglow and exists just for a very few seconds. It's very hard to make that light work on a piece of film, but it's very nice to be able to swim within it.

All water contains different qualities of light. I grew up along the coast that has maybe the worst water

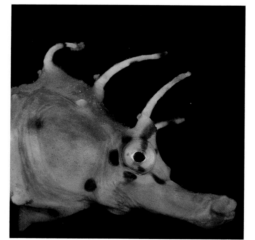

Yellow sea horse. New Zealand.
David Doubilet.

in the world, the New Jersey coast. If you go out to sea there, the water does get clearer because it gets tendrils of the Gulf Stream coming in. So sometimes the visibility pushes up to 60, 80, 100 feet, but inshore along this bleak coast, punctuated by jetties, the water is a mixing bowl with patches of clear water, patches of dirty water, patches of silt-laden water, and patches of plankton blooms in the summer. The patches come and go, and they blow in and out like fog.

Sometimes that's terribly exciting, but it's also what made me appreciate really clear water. When it's clear, even in New Jersey in the shallows you begin to see spidery tracings of light on the sand.

Light can be a constant in the sea. In other words, it's a great big blue diffuser, but you're inside the diffuser. When the sun goes behind a cloud, the sea goes from a joyous blue to a military gray in a second—and I then have to scramble with shutter-speed settings to make things work. The blue also plays enormous tricks—it absorbs the red. In less than 3 feet of water, much of the red color is gone. If you wear a red shirt, it turns maroon in 10 feet of water and by 50 feet in the clearest ocean that red shirt is black. If you cut yourself in 50 feet of water your blood is green.

With a strobe you take bottled sunlight into the sea, and it restores the whole spectrum of colors. In an underwater world that had been full of blue-green monotonous light there are unbelievable colors, colors not found in a Kandinsky canvas or a parrot's wing— reds, pinks, yellows that take chromium yellow a step beyond, combinations of dark purples, and darker blues. It's unbelievable stuff. This blast of bottled sunlight restores the spectrum, and the colors leap out and glow. I've photographed what I thought was obsidian black, and it turned out to be crimson, or sometimes just obsidian black. The sea is full of these kinds of secrets, and it constantly surprises me.

Jellyfish go through two stages of life. First, they are polyps, then as adults they are known as medusae, perhaps because of their long, waving deadly arms. Medusa, one of the three gorgons of Greek myth, had hair made of serpents and could turn men to stone. With reason, the sting of the jellyfish is equally feared. Their stinging nematocysts can deliver a deadly blow to small fish and a nasty jolt to a human.
Japan. David Doubilet.

DR. ROGER PAYNE

Founder and President of the Whale Conservation Institute

The idea that some whale populations may be recovering is the most exciting thing of all in my research. Everybody talks wistfully about how the Great Plains looked when they were covered with game and about how life on earth was thousands of years ago. The truth of the matter is that we could have returned to life as it was long ago if we had just left things alone and allowed them to return to normal. By now, though, we have to protect many of our wildlife species and coddle them and make sure that they have the opportunity to thrive.

There used to be right whales, now the rarest whale species of all, off the northeast coast of the United States. They were off every beach at certain times of the year. You could walk along the beach in the company of a whale in the same way you still can in Argentina.

There's no way to describe how that feels. If you have the experience with your children, as I have, you can't describe how that bonds your family. It's a real experience. It's not a fantasy-contrived, clever robot experience. Every fiber of your being, every neuron, feels natural in the circumstances because that experience is what the last three million years of evolution of human lineage have been working toward. You feel absolutely "with it." You know exactly what you're doing and where you are, and things speak to you the way they never do through a television set or through any sort of modern computer-age trickery. The experience of walking in the company of whales could be had again. It's very simple. Just protect the whales, and they will come back. Once they've returned you can enjoy them.

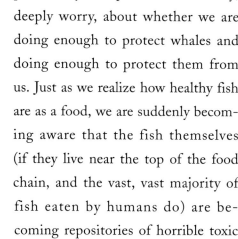

Beluga whale. Vancouver.
James Gritz.

However, there is an insidious background worry that's slowly moving forward from the shadows into the light. This background worry is the fact that we are slowly polluting the seas, and this process has a cumulative effect. There seems to be enough stuff out there to threaten the existence of the fish in the sea. As the toxic stuff moves up the food chain in increased concentrations, it will cause terrible problems for whales, weakening their immune systems and so on, as we have seen happen in other mammals. Eventually, it could bring whales to extinction.

People have to worry about that possibility. People need to worry, deeply worry, about whether we are doing enough to protect whales and doing enough to protect them from us. Just as we realize how healthy fish are as a food, we are suddenly becoming aware that the fish themselves (if they live near the top of the food chain, and the vast, vast majority of fish eaten by humans do) are becoming repositories of horrible toxic material. Therefore, they may in fact no longer be safe to eat. That's a selfish reason for doing something about the oceans—to protect our own food resources—but it's a reason.

Beyond the need for food, I think that something does have to be done to protect whales. If we don't protect them, then I don't have much hope for them—not at least for the toothed whales which feed on fish that are high on the food chain. Unless some process we don't yet know about removes the toxins and saves us, then I think the prospect for whales may be very bleak.

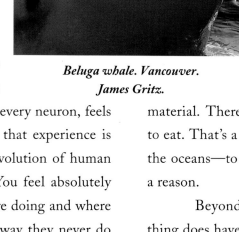

Among his many accomplishments in the study of whales, Roger Payne is credited, along with colleague Scott McVay, with discovering that the sounds humpback whales make are actually songs. Alaska. James Gritz.

Chapter Three
INTERACTIONS AMONG SPECIES

In well-functioning human communities, every person has a job to do, a role to play in a pattern of life that can be quite complex. The same is true of natu-ral ecosystems, but they are more complex in that they contain many different species and many different individuals within those species.

In any ecosystem, living organisms must compete with each other for the particular resources they need: space, nutrients, food, and sometimes light and oxygen. Most species have coped with competition over the course of their evolution by developing ways to live and to gather food that set them apart from other species or allow them the flexibility to exploit a wide range of food and housing. In this way, an ecosystem can support a number of different species.

Some species team up with other species in a process called symbiosis. Generally, one species gains protection while the other gains a more reliable food source. A species of crab that lives near the Seychelles in the Indian Ocean wears a small stinging anemone on each claw to shove in the face of threatening predators. Gaudy clown fish have established a relationship with other kinds of stinging anemones; both species get more food, and the clown fish gets protection.

In the ocean, as on land, communication must occur between individuals and between species. Messages are signaled in various ways. These include sounds; broadcast chemicals, which other organisms detect; and appearance—colors, designs, shapes, and movements.

Bluehead wrasses cleaning a queen triggerfish. There are more than thirty species of cleaner fish, shrimp, and crabs. Fish such as the queen triggerfish will execute an intricate behavior pattern to request cleaning services. Cleaners then move with impunity over their client, cleaning even the eyes, mouth, and gills. Occasionally, a false cleaner—a fish with a similar color pattern to a cleaner fish—will sneak in and grab a mouthful of healthy flesh. Little Cayman. Robert E. Barber.

Many species of fish and invertebrates also signal to others by making their own light: bioluminescence, or phosphorescence, as it is sometimes called. It is used to augment other visual signals or to replace them in the dark of the deep abyss. Also, elaborate patterns of luminescent spots often distinguish species, such as squid. Some fish use bioluminescent flashlights and lighted lures in hunting for food.

above: *Stingrays. The stingers on a stingray are located in one or more venomous barbs on the tail. Though a sting can be very painful, it is rarely fatal to humans. Stingrays use their stinging tails only in defense and not to subdue prey.*
Cocos Island, Costa Rica. Marty Snyderman.

left: *Water filters out the long red wavelengths in the light spectrum. The longnose hawk fish appears vividly red in this picture, but to predators or prey it would appear maroon or even black. The longnose hawk fish is hiding in soft coral of the same color— a typical daytime resting place for these fish. At night, the hawk fish is almost invisible—a stealth fish—and it can be the hunter. Most red fishes are nocturnal predators.*
Fiji. Scott Frier.

overleaf: *Shrimp larva on sea cucumber. Scott Frier.*

BIOLUMINESCENCE

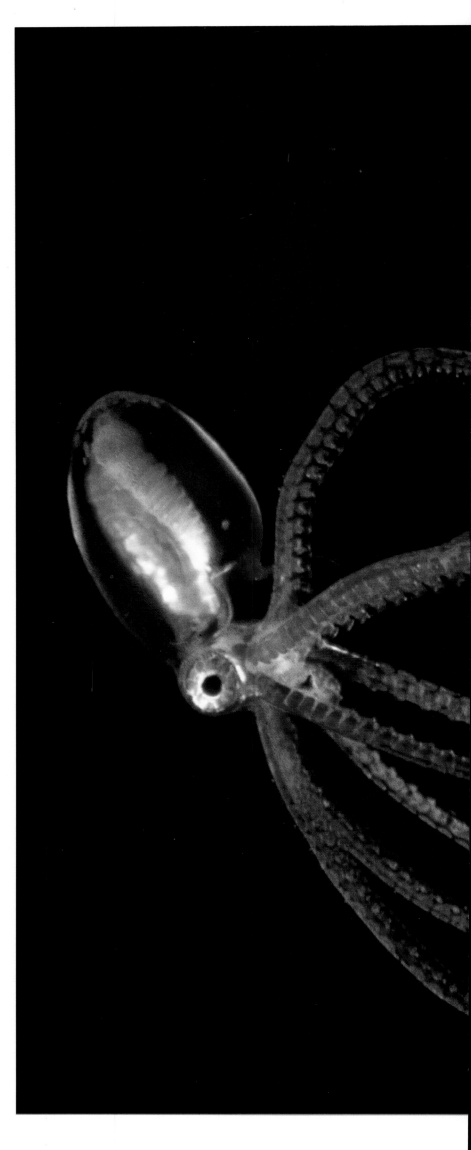

Bioluminescence, the biological conversion of chemical energy into light, can be found in a relatively small number of land species: lightning bugs, glowworms, and some mushrooms. It is far more general in the ocean, and has evolved independently in almost every major group of marine animals as well as in bacteria and in some microalgae.

In the chemical mechanism that produces light, an enzyme called luciferase catalyzes a chemical reaction between organic molecules called luciferins and oxygen. During this reaction, bits of extra energy are excited and released as light. The light is called cold light because nothing burns; only about 1 percent of the energy is lost as heat. Bioluminescence is thus the most efficient form of light production known.

Bioluminescent light is nearly always green or blue, the wavelengths best able to penetrate seawater. Intensity varies from one species to another, and even within a single individual. Animals usually use the mechanism only in the dark, but bioluminescence can also be stimulated by physical disturbances. Some species produce flashes, others a steady and constant light; yet others can regulate the light they make according to their needs.

In several species, the entire organism emits light, while in others the light may be contained in special pockets or organs called photophores. Some crustaceans, fish, and squid and octopus have developed these organs, and their structure tends to be fairly constant: a lens in front of the light source and a concave reflector behind it.

Some animals use the light in feeding, either as a lure to attract other animals or as a lantern to illuminate the surrounding waters. The numerous

Pelagic octopus. Many open-ocean cephalopods—squids, octopuses, and cuttlefish—display bioluminescence. Typically, this occurs in the form of elaborate patterns of light-producing photophores on the cephalopod's body and tentacles.
Open Pacific Ocean. Chris Newbert.

species of anglerfish of the deep sea extend an often very long luminous lure on the end of a stalk in front of their mouths. Another type of deep-sea fish lets a similar stalked light hang down or forward; the stalk mimics the form of some kinds of illuminated crustaceans. The fish dines on the other predators attracted to the lure. Other types of predatory fish hunt using intense light from large luminous organs near their eyes. These lights can usually be turned on and off at will.

Bioluminescence is used by several animals to hide from or confuse potential predators. Many deep-sea prawns discharge large clouds of bioluminescence when startled. Sudden flashes of light in the face can scare a predator away. One species of jellyfish has lights on both tentacles and body. When threatened, the jellyfish turns off the body lights but continues to illuminate the tentacles. These attract the predators, who devour a mouthful of stinging tentacles while the jellyfish—whose lost extremities will grow back in time—escapes. Many deep-sea fish, crustaceans, and squid sport elaborate arrays of photophores on their undersides. The light simulates the natural levels of sunlight that reach those depths,

above: The flashlight fish produces bright blue-green light as a result of a symbiotic relationship with bioluminescent bacteria that live in pouches below the fish's eyes and gain nourishment from the fish's blood vessels. Flashlight fish use their lights to attract their planktonic prey at night. By rotating the whole organ inward or outward, they can turn the light on and off to confuse potential predators. In a tactic known as blink and run, the flashlight fish swims one way with its lights on, then blinks them off and swims the other way. It can do this up to seventy-five times a minute. The flashlight fish's light is the brightest in the ocean.
Grand Cayman. Courtney Platt.

right: Pygmy sweepers have bioluminescent organs on each side of their bodies.
Red Sea. Chris Newbert.

overleaf: Hermit crab. With their soft abdomens, hermit crabs are required to borrow shells for protection. They trade up to new, larger shells as they grow.
Caribbean. Scott Frier.

thus rendering the animal virtually invisible to upward-looking predators.

Finally, many animals use photophores to identify themselves to others of their species. Some fish, squid, and octopus sport very elaborate light patterns. These are probably useful in courtship displays or for establishing territories.

Adversarial relationships among species are common in nature; at one time or another every species is involved in a conflict with other species. In symbiosis, a directly opposite process occurs: two species associate because they are better off together than they would be apart.

Coral reefs offer many examples of symbiotic organisms. To begin with, there are the corals themselves, which have established an intimate symbiotic relationship with the microalgae that live within their tissue. Corals are small colonial animals—each individual is called a "polyp"—that secrete calcium carbonate houses and filter-feed on microscopic plankton. As the polyps die, their skeletons become part of the reef, and a new layer of living coral grows over them. Of the particles that the polyps filter out of the water, primarily the animals are eaten. But during the process of filter feeding certain microalgae are taken in by the corals and then incorporated as symbiotic zooxanthellae into the living tissue of the coral. There the zooxanthellae lose their locomotive flagella, and exist simply as photosynthesizing cells, contributing their production of excess oxygen and carbohydrates to the host coral. In turn, the coral provides the microalgae with carbon dioxide and nitrogen in its waste products, and protects them from other filter feeders. Without zooxanthellae, the polyps could not survive—and thus there would be no coral reefs.

Meanwhile, the dense packing of microalgae that results from the symbiotic relationship between coral polyps and zooxanthellae enriches the surrounding waters with oxygen, and this helps support

Goggle-eyes schooling over table and staghorn corals. By day, the goggle-eyes assume a reddish color and stay close to the cover of coral. At night, however, they become silvery and leave the cover of the reef to hunt large zooplankton in open waters. Coral reefs are prime areas for symbiotic relationships, probably because such a wide variety of life is densely packed into the reef ecosystem. Great Barrier Reef, Australia. Fred Bavendam.

the large animal community that develops around the reefs.

The giant clam, another coral reef animal that lives in shallow tropical waters, has also developed a symbiotic relationship with the tiny zooxanthellae. Giant clams may be more than three feet across and weigh as much as 500 pounds. They lie on the bottom with their shells opened in such a way that a layer of living tissue spreads over the shell edge. Because this layer is exposed to water and light, it can include algae cells. Although the clam is a filter feeder, it somehow manages to avoid eating the algae; instead, the zooxanthellae pass into the outer layer tissue, where they photosynthesize and share nutrients with the clam.

Several species of crab place other animals on their shells for camouflage and defense. The sponge crab plucks fragments of sponge and secures them to its shell. In time, the sponge grows over most of the crab, concealing it from predators, most of which find sponges unpalatable. The sponge, for its part, gains mobility and a greater choice of food, which it filters from the water.

One of the most-photographed symbiotic duos in coral reefs are the colorful sea anemone and the clown fish. The clown fish lives happily among the anemone's stinging tentacles without fear that the otherwise voracious anemone will eat it. The relationship is individualized: the fish is immune only to the host anemone and not any others, not

above left: *Pom-pom crab. This pom-pom crab has attached stinging anemones to each of its claws. It can then wave the anemones in the face of potential predators. The crab is also carrying a mass of small, red eggs under its torso. Tropical Indo-Pacific. Lynn Funkhouser.*

above: *French grunt and isopod parasite. In this example of parasitic symbiosis, the French grunt is an unwilling host to an isopod. Using their hooks, isopods sometimes attach themselves directly to fish, pierce the skin, and feed on the blood. Caribbean. Scott Frier.*

right: *The lion's mane jellyfish has a mutually beneficial relationship with juvenile jackfish. Young jacks are immune to the lion's mane sting and find a safe haven while growing up within the protection of its tentacles. Larger fish are attracted to the shiny jacks and chase them into the tentacles, whereupon the potential predators are stung and consumed by the jellyfish. British Virgin Islands. Scott Frier.*

even of the same species. Conversely, the anemone will eat any strange clown fish that comes within reach of its sting. A symbiotic partnership starts with a clown fish tentatively contacting a few anemone tentacles at a time. After a while, it builds up an immunity, apparently produced by a protective slime coating on its skin. Meanwhile, the fish benefits from the anemone's protection and from the scraps of food it scavenges from the anemone's meals. The gain for its partner is that the colorful little fish both cleans the anemone and attracts predators to its sting and grasp.

Cleaning is important in the marine environment, and is the basis of numerous symbiotic relationships. For example, some species of shrimp

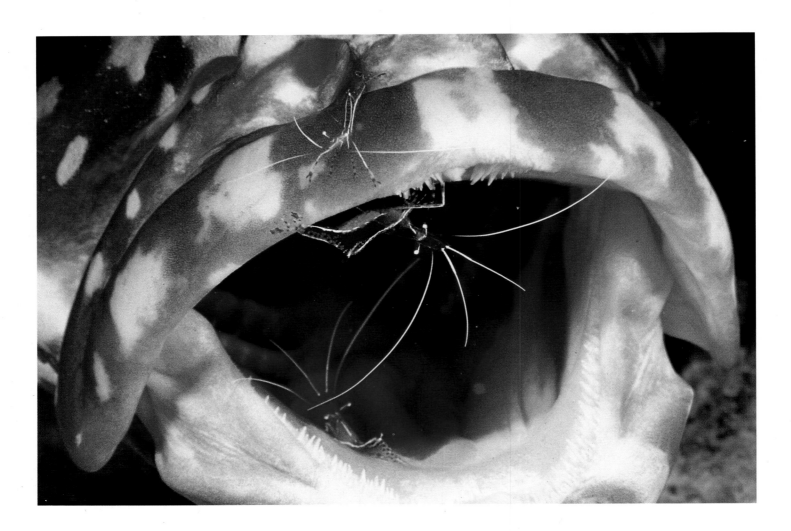

Nassau grouper with Peterson's cleaning shrimp. The grouper could easily vacuum these shrimp into its gullet, but instead it allows them remarkable access as they go about their work. Cleaning shrimp approach the grouper's eyes, gills, and other sensitive areas to remove parasites, diseased skin, and the like. Providenciales, Turks & Caicos. Doug Perrine.

clean the gills and mouths of fish and remove parasites from their skin. The shrimp advertise to potential clients by dancing and waving their antennae. Fish look for these cleaners, even wait in line to be served. Instead of being eaten, the shrimp have a nearly continuous supply of food delivered to them.

Numerous species of small cleaner fish also advertise their location using color and movement. Larger fish, including sharks and moray eels, will seek the cleaner fish and wait in long lines at the service station. When it's their turn to be serviced, they will contort their bodies in surprising ways to facilitate the removal of particles and debris from their mouths, gills, and bodies. The term cleaning service station is quite accurate, as cleaner fish do not move around much. Fish that use their services learn where the stations are, and come back to them repeatedly.

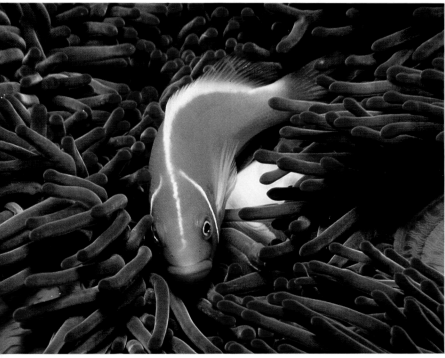

above: *Though these remoras are hitchhiking on a manta ray, remoras also hitch on sharks, turtles, mammals, and sometimes ships. They are the only fish with sucking disks, actually modified dorsal fins, which they use to create a vacuum by which they attach themselves to their hosts. This vacuum can be extremely powerful—in some areas fishermen bait lines with remoras and wait for the remoras to attach themselves to a fish.*
Hawaii. Marty Snyderman.

left: *Anemone fish and anemone. The anemone fish typically establishes a relationship with an anemone to the clear benefit of both. Setting up shop is a careful process in which the fish slowly acclimatizes itself to the sting of the anemone of its choice. The fish develops an immunity as a result of repeated small doses of the anemone's sting. The anemone fish then lives permanently among the anemone's tentacles. Would-be predators are attracted to the brightly colored fish, and when they move in to feed, the anemone immobilizes and consumes them. Thus the anemone fish is saved and the anemone gets fed. The anemone fish may also get a few scraps of leftover food from the anemone.*
Solomon Islands. Burt Jones & Maurine Shimlock.

overleaf: *Scarlet lady shrimp cleaning parasites from queen angel.*
Bahamas. Doug Perrine.

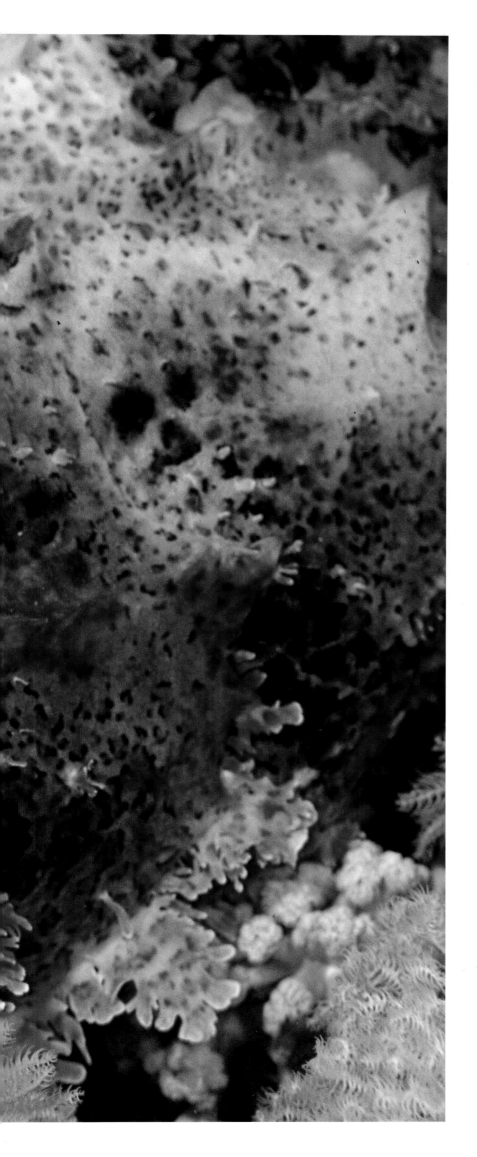

COLORATION, CAMOUFLAGE, AND MIMICRY

Animals display characteristic colors and patterns to identify themselves to others of their species and sometimes to different species. Just as on land, a distinctive appearance often attracts mates. It can also attract companions in those species that school. A few species actually socialize with other species, and several animals need to advertise themselves to possible symbiotic associates.

Some fish flare colorfully marked fins to signal friendship to potential mates or hostility to interlopers. A number of invertebrates actually change body color, either to send messages or to match their background. Octopuses, squid, and cuttlefish do this most amazingly, and very rapidly.

Many noxious species are brightly colored to advertise themselves to predators, who quickly learn to avoid them. The brilliant colors of nudibranchs and of sea anemones signal unpleasant, stinging mouthfuls.

Some animals have evolved color patterns, shapes, and behaviors that mimic those of the particularly unpalatable species. The filefish, for instance, both looks and swims like the noxious puffer. Mimicry is also used to lure prey: some fish species have evolved coloration and behavior that mimic cleaner-fish species; when larger fish come for cleaning, the mimic nibbles pieces out of their fins instead.

Camouflage is also very common in the ocean, and often involves shape as well as color. Many fish and invertebrates are colored to match their natural surroundings. A number of bottom-dwelling flatfish, for example, can settle onto the

Scorpion fish. With a remarkable ability to mimic color, patterns, and textures, the scorpion fish is nearly invisible while it lies waiting to ambush prey. The venomous poison in the scorpion fish's spines, used only for defense, affects both the nervous system and the blood of the fish's attacker.
Red Sea. Chris Newbert.

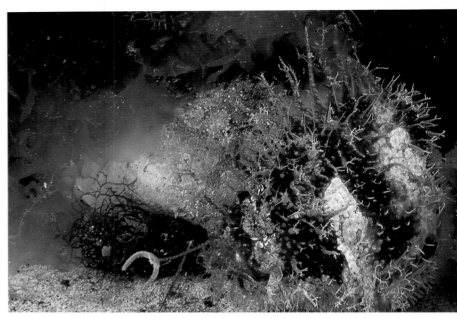

The tasseled angler fish deceives in two ways. First, it is so well camouflaged it appears to be an innocuous clump of seaweed. Second, it dangles a small, worm-shaped lure, which it wiggles vigorously to attract prey. The angler fish is a voracious eater and can suck prey into its gaping mouth. Edithburg, Australia. Fred Bavendam.

sediments and all but disappear into the background. Blending into the background is also an advantage to a predator. Thus, moray eels show dull and often irregular patterns of dark and light neutral colors, making them less obvious to other animals as they lie in wait among the shadows of the coral.

The most bizarre-looking animals are colored and shaped to blend in amid a background of seaweeds. In tropical waters, for instance, scorpion fishes and frogfish have fleshy tassels or warts that resemble seaweed fronds. A number even have algae growing on them. In the Sargasso Sea, among the drifting rafts of the brown seaweed sargassum, lives an entire community of animals that look just like, or blend into, the sargassum itself: fish, crabs, nudibranchs, shrimp, all are golden or mottled brown, and some sport mock foliage.

In open-ocean waters, fish often school for protection. The sheer numbers of fish in a school ensure that, when attacked, most will survive, because predators have a difficult time singling out individuals. If a predator simply blindly lunges at a school, it will usually fail to catch anything. Some schooling species, however, also rely upon disruptive coloration. For example, a pattern of vertical bars on many moving bodies makes identifying an individual fish impossible.

above: *The signal goby appears to be a contradiction in colors. Although its mottled brown body blends well with the background, the brown and yellow spots on its fins advertise its presence like bull's-eyes. That may, in fact, be how they function. If a predator attempts to bite near what appear to be eyes, it will simply get a mouthful of fin. When the signal goby is seen in profile the spots look like the eyes of a much larger fish and may therefore serve to scare off predators as well. Solomon Islands. Chris Newbert.*

left: *The well-camouflaged stargazer spends much of its life concealed on the bottom waiting for prey to wander within range. The Greeks called the stargazer the "holy fish" because it appeared to be contemplating the heavens. Red Sea. Chris Newbert.*

overleaf: *Blue-ringed octopus. Australia. Alex Kerstitch.*

COMPETITION

Two or more species will compete when their needs overlap. No two species will occupy the same niche in an ecosystem, but they may require the same type of food or space. When the competition is relatively even, or when the advantage swings back and forth between the species, the two species can coexist in dynamic equilibrium. If one species is consistently more successful than the other, the losing species will disappear from the ecosystem or else take a minor role and maintain a very small population.

A species that is inefficient in utilizing resources may compensate for its disadvantage in other ways—with a more successful reproductive strategy, for example. Environmental factors may also prevent the elimination of the inferior species. Removal of a portion of the population of the dominant species will prolong the coexistence of competitors. Periodic storms across a coastal bottom, for example, remove a percentage of the community, providing open space and reduced competition. For a time, at least, this will benefit the weaker competitors. Repeated disturbances can thus prevent the competitive exclusion of weaker species.

The introduction of predators into the ecosystem will produce similar results. If the predator preys on the dominant species, or even both species, the population of the stronger species will be kept in check, allowing the weaker species to survive. Predation is a particularly important influence on species diversity in coastal ecosystems.

The result of dynamically balanced competition is greater species diversity in the ecosystem. It also means that the community structure fluctuates as first one species, then another, is favored by a particular environmental situation.

California sea lions. Male sea lions have harems and push, bite, and bang each other in battles for territory. Once a sea lion has won its territory, which can extend from land into the water, it will breed with all the females within the territory, but the females are free to go to other territories as well.
Galápagos. Doug Perrine.

Some changes can be permanent. In one temperate intertidal community, research scientists removed a noted predator, a starfish, to see what would happen to the rest of the community. Very quickly, one of the starfish's prey species, mussels, won out over several other species, all of which disappeared. Furthermore, once most of the mussels grew to a size too large for the starfish to eat, reintroducing the predator starfish did not reverse the situation. The predators could not remove a sufficient quantity of the mussel population to allow other competing species to reestablish themselves.

above: *Spanish shawl nudibranch and anemone. Although it appears that the nudibranch is being consumed by the anemone, the nudibranch is the one on the attack. The nudibranch is able to eat the anemone's tentacles without letting the stinging nematocysts discharge. In fact, it is able to incorporate the ingested nematocysts into its own tissue as part of its defense against predators. When a predator bites the nudibranch it will get a stinging mouthful of anemone nematocysts.*
Monterey Bay, California. Roger Hess.

right: *Tidal zones are regions of intense interspecies competition, as numerous types of plants and animals fight for precious real estate. Intertidal zones on steep-sloped rocky shores are usually marked by bands of color that reflect the predominance of certain plants or animals at different levels.*
Pacific Northwest. Nancy Sefton.

overleaf: *Pacific giant octopus scavenging dead spiny dogfish shark. Campbell River, British Columbia. Fred Bavendam.*

RED TIDES

Marine microalgae normally live in communities composed of a large number of species competing for light and nutrients. This competition generally results in a dynamic balance among the various species, with a continuous jostling for dominance. Frequently, the competition involves chemical warfare, with one species releasing substances that impede the growth of other species.

Environmental conditions sometimes favor a particular alga, which may bloom so intensely that it virtually wipes out all the other phytoplankton species nearby. When this happens, the water around the bloom can take on the color of the victorious alga. In some famous and recurring incidents, the micro-algae have a reddish color; hence the name red tide.

The algae most frequently implicated in red tides are several species of dinoflagellates that produce toxins. One algal neurotoxin will kill fish or any other vertebrate that eats it, including humans who eat shellfish that have eaten the noxious dinoflagellates. Paralytic shellfish poisoning, as it is called, has been known for centuries and is a frequent threat during summer months along some coastlines. Other species of algae produce other kinds of toxins that cause symptoms such as diarrhea and neurological disorders. Given the chemical battles that occur among species of phytoplankton, it is not surprising that many algae blooms are poisonous or toxic.

Scientists have identified a number of algae species of different colors that commonly appear in solo blooms. Some are toxic, some not. Though they are still generally called red tides, a particular bloom might be called locally by its true color—green tide or brown tide. Scientists have begun to use a more general term: harmful algal blooms, or HAB.

Coastal regions are important breeding, nursery, and food-producing areas. The toxins often present in red tides can have far-reaching consequences on other organisms and ecosystems. South Georgia Island, Antarctic. Frans Lanting.

Many scientists studying red tides believe that as a result of nutrient pollution there has been a significant global rise in toxic algal blooms. Sewage and fertilizer runoff, containing large quantities of nitrogen and phosphorus, flows into estuaries and coastal waters, causing phytoplankton blooms so dense that grazing cannot keep growth in check. The dead, unconsumed phytoplankton cells fall to the bottom, where they decompose, using up the oxygen that the bottom community needs in order to survive. Thus, even a nontoxic algal bloom may severely damage the ecosystem.

Scientists are reporting more blooms, in more places, than ever before: they are also identifying new bloom species. Yet the logical response—reducing the pollution flowing into coastal waters—is difficult to implement, because it would involve unpopular additional operating costs for industry, agriculture, and general sewage disposal. Until the effect of pollution on HABs has been proved beyond all doubt, the policy makers and regulators in a position to control nutrient pollution can be counted on to do little or nothing.

above: *The United States' East Coast is commonly afflicted by red tides. These harmful algal blooms typically occur in the summer and may last for weeks.*
New Jersey. Michael Baytoff.

left: *Dolphin killed in 1987 die-off. Bottlenose dolphins were linked to red tides after a mysterious die-off in the summer of 1987 off the United States' East Coast. The cause of the die-off is a controversial issue: according to one theory the dolphins died after exposure to the toxins produced by red tides. Another theory holds that the dolphins were done in by high levels of other pollutants that weakened their immune systems.*
New Jersey. Michael Baytoff.

DR. EUGENIE CLARK

Professor of Zoology at the University of Maryland

Ever since I was a child, I have been interested in looking at fishes in aquariums—whether in my home or at the public aquarium. I dreamed about being underwater with them, and today that's what I do. Now, though, I'm able to observe them with a trained eye.

I discovered one little fish through serendipity when I was studying garden eels while scuba-diving in the Red Sea. Photographer David Doubilet and I would set up an underwater blind in which we would hide to shoot photos and observe. To pass the time, as we sat in the blind waiting for the garden eels to come out of their holes, I would try a yoga technique of not breathing much or just try to rest and observe the sand. As a result, I started to see wonderful things in the sand. One was a new species, the Tricky Nicky fish (*Trichonotus nikii*), which I named after my son Niki. I just looked at it, flabbergasted to see a fish I'd never seen before.

The ocean unfolds its surprises to those who watch and wait. When I'm observing one fish, I'll wait and wait to see what will happen, and out of the corner of my eye I might see something I never expected to see, and I might see fish staring back. I call them Houdinis, or ninja fish. You look here and there, and you see these eyes. You notice that hundreds of eyes are observing you. I don't mind. I'm watching them so why can't they watch me?

After a while they get used to you, and they go about their own business, doing whatever that particular species does. I like to watch them from the time they wake up to when they go to bed at night. I get a picture

Red-lipped batfish. Cocos Island.
Birgitte Wilms.

of them throughout the day and begin to get a better understanding of their behavior.

I once came across a razorfish—a species that has a reputation for being very shy—that came up to me and ate the yolks of hard-boiled eggs out of my hand. She was the dominant female in the harem, and when she approached me the male would stay in the background. Razorfish were not known to mate in the afternoon, but one day the male began coming closer as she was eating. She turned around, mated, and then resumed eating.

I called her Gill, because she had a spot on her gill. Eventually, she appeared to be changing into a male (razorfish are hermaphrodites), and I asked David Shen, with whom I was working, to catch her so we could study her gonads. He used an egg to lure her into a plastic bag, but then didn't have the heart to close it. I felt relieved: I realized I didn't want to kill her either.

I suddenly asked myself, "Why do we have to kill these animals?" I felt there was no reason I couldn't devote the rest of my life to studying fishes year after year, going back and seeing how they grow, how they mate, how they live in territories. I would let nature decide when they die. Since then, I have never killed a fish.

Studying the ocean is a wonderful experience. All my life I've found that whenever you delve into a subject in detail you discover new things. People ask me how I've been able to make so many discoveries, and I tell them that in part it's because I concentrate on what interests me. I love the beauty of the ocean, but I most enjoy concentrating on one fish. Most people swim over all those wonders and don't even know they're there.

*Eugenie Clark discovered this fish while sitting with David Doubilet in a photographer's blind on the Red Sea floor. She named it the Tricky Nicky (**Trichonotus nikii**) in honor of her son Niki.*
Red Sea. David Doubilet.

KATHRYN FULLER

President of the World Wildlife Fund

It was somewhat by happenstance that I began studying marine ecology. I had signed up to pursue a master's in ecology to add to my experience in practicing natural resource law and found myself drawn toward the marine world. Not only was the course work fascinating, but the program also provided the impetus for me to learn to scuba-dive and spend a summer doing coral reef research in the Virgin Islands. What a revelation that was. From my first exploration underwater, I began to appreciate the richness, beauty, and complexity of a realm almost invisible to us land dwellers.

And what a contrast to my earlier experiences doing fieldwork in Africa! The remarkable panorama of African wildlife was inspiring, indeed, but it felt almost familiar—like watching a movie whose plot you know. The marine world came as such a wonderful surprise to me and, as a result, was absolutely mesmerizing. I found I could spend hours watching shrimp emerge from their sand mounds and small damsel fish police their territories.

Nudibranch. California Channel Islands.
Marty Snyderman.

With enhanced appreciation of the incredible complexity of the marine environment came appreciation of its fragility as well. Ever since, I have been determined to continue my ocean explorations—to snorkel and dive, perhaps even go down in a submersible—and to do what I can to protect the marine world.

We humans view the world largely through a terrestrial lens, yet in some respects the marine environment is even more threatened than the terrestrial. We have assumed that we can abuse the ocean even more than we abuse resources on the land. Because many marine species are invisible to most people, most of the threats are, too.

We all hear about the escalating losses of forests in many parts of the world; we hear little about comparable marine emergencies. A biologist recently told me that nearly 80 percent of the grasses in the Chesapeake Bay disappeared in the late 1970s and 1980s, and, with them, critical habitat for a host of fish, crabs, and other species. If that sort of disaster had happened on land, the public outcry would have been tremendous. Educating the public about the threats to our marine systems and countering the impression that the oceans' riches are inexhaustible are major challenges for conservationists.

We still have much to learn about many of the species in the oceans and the different systems they inhabit. Consider the fact that whole new groups of organisms have been discovered in deep-ocean vents in the last twenty years, flourishing independent of sunlight and unlike any others we know.

It is a truism perhaps, but the oceans are the last frontier. We know less about them in some respects than we do about space. The oceans are more a scientific frontier, more a frontier in terms of the rigors of exploration, and more a psychic frontier. And it is a frontier we may lose before we even have a chance to explore it.

A terrestrial scientist by training, Kathryn Fuller was introduced
to the beauties of the undersea world while in graduate school.
She has done a great deal of diving on coral reefs and hopes to dive
soon in the underwater cathedral of a kelp forest.
San Clemente Island, California. Marty Snyderman.

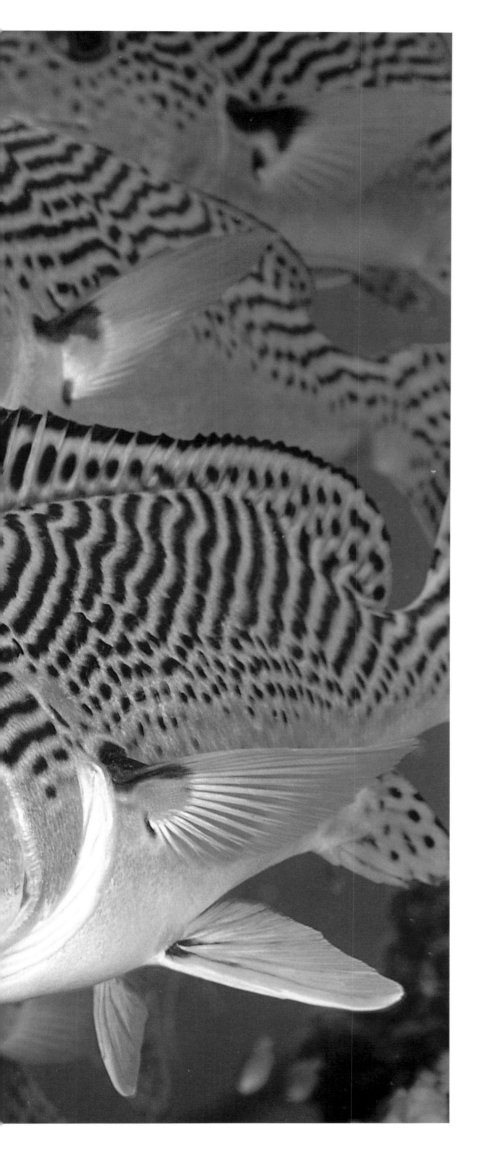

Chapter Four

MARINE BIODIVERSITY

Biodiversity is nature's way of assuring the adaptability and survival of life on Earth. There are three types of biodiversity: genetic diversity, the range of genetic information found among the individuals in a species; species diversity, the variety of species found in an ecosystem; and ecological diversity, the variety of ecosystems on Earth.

Variety is the key to survival. Genetic diversity allows a species to adapt to a broader range of environmental conditions and increase its chances of survival. Similarly, diversity in species increases the adaptability of an ecosystem. And a large number of fully functioning ecosystems, each operating within particular ranges of environmental conditions, increases the general adaptability of life to continued global change.

When seeking to protect biodiversity on Earth, it is not enough to preserve only ecosystems with large numbers of species; the key is preserving a range of ecosystems that can thrive under a variety of environmental conditions. Thus, while coral reefs harbor a great number of species, the polar seas, with far fewer species, are also important, because they represent a community of species and a pool of genes that can adapt to conditions very different from those favored by the coral reef gene pool.

Species and ecosystems do not exist in isolation. As a species living on Earth, humans must fit themselves into natural systems and take steps to ensure these systems' survival. To protect ourselves and our descendants, we must protect not only other species but also habitats and large ecosystems, both on land and in the ocean.

Lined sweetlips over a coral reef. The ocean brims with life, and fish account for more than half the vertebrate species alive today. Fish are divided into four major subgroups; bony fishes, by far the largest subgroup, include more than 20,000 species. Australia. Doug Perrine.

overleaf: *Dusky cardinal fish and brittle star in tube sponge. Cayman Islands. Al Grotell.*

COASTAL ECOSYSTEMS

The coastal zone encompasses all waters near land. It extends outward from the shore to the edge of the continental shelf, and reaches inward as far as the highest tide level and into estuaries and up rivers as far as these are under the influence of tides.

Within the coastal zone one finds a variety of interconnected ecosystems: the rocky shore communities along the open coast and the coasts of some estuaries; the estuaries themselves, characterized by a mixture of salt and fresh water; wetlands, which lie at the margins of some estuaries; giant kelp beds, which lie in deeper waters offshore; and reefs.

ROCKY SHORES

Cliffs, crags, promontories, stony beaches, and rocks that tumble into the sea—all are home to a splendid variety of ocean plants and animals. We can find dwellers in this rocky community at the highest reaches of the tides, even to the limits of the surf sprays, as well as down below the tides, where the rocks end and subtidal sandy bottom sediments take over.

This is an ecosystem of extremes: its shores are alternately bathed in water and exposed to dry air. The constant waves pound some areas; others are protected by curved shores, by cliffs, or by the angle at which they face the waves. Even more protected are tidal pools, basins that flood when the tide rises and then hold water after the tide ebbs. Tidal pools are oases for intertidal life that would otherwise dry out when exposed to air.

All of these rocky spaces are rich in species, especially at the lower tide levels, where the rocks teem with life. The hard, irregular, unshifting surface

Harbor seal in kelp forest. Seals split their time between land and sea, although they are far more graceful and agile in the water than on land. Seals can dive to depths of more than 100 feet, but they like to stay close to shore and often rest on sandbars and rocky islets. Harbor seals sometimes venture inland up rivers. Monterey Bay, California. David Doubilet.

Sea anemones and coralline algae. These sea anemones are huddling in the last remnants of water left by the receding tide in the tidal pool. They have retained water in pools around their mouths and have also begun to fold in their tentacles. By contrast, the barnacles exposed to air have retracted into their houses. Olympic National Park, Washington. Thomas Wiewandt.

is ideal for those plants and animals that attach themselves and wait for nutrients and food to be washed over them. Barnacles in profusion weld themselves to the rocks. Looking more like flowers than the predatory animals they are, anemones firmly grasp the bottom as the tide flows in and out. Mussels spin their sticky threads to glue themselves down. And, of course, seaweeds abound: from delicate, red, feathery forms to the larger and coarser brown kelp; some spread leafy fronds, others are more linear.

More mobile bottom-dwelling animals, such as crabs, starfish, chitons, sea cucumbers, sea hares, and various marine snails, roam over the rocks, seaweed, and barnacles. When the tide goes out, it drapes seaweeds across the exposed rocks, and cover is thereby provided for many animals.

The waves energize this already active environment. At low tide, seaweeds are exposed to increased sunlight, and they are continuously bathed in sprays

of water and dissolved nutrients. These seaweeds therefore grow rapidly. Grazing snails, limpets, urchins, and other munching herbivores take advantage of the abundant food supply. Meanwhile, filter feeders, such as barnacles and mussels, are washed in waters rich in microalgae that continuously refill their baskets with food.

On the outermost intertidal rocks, where the surf is roughest, we can find a community of seaweeds perfectly adapted to the environment. While its holdfast (a rootlike system) keeps the sea palm (*Postelsia*) attached to the rocks, its fat, supple stalk lets it bend back and forth with the action of the waves. Thus, the sea palm's crown of tough leaflike fronds can take full advantage of sunlight and the ever-refreshed solution of nutrients. This plant literally thrives on being beaten up.

In sharp contrast, the tidal pools above the low-tide line are a slower, quieter world, offering the

Goose barnacles are well adapted to living in the intertidal environment because they simply close up their houses when exposed to the air. When submerged, they open up and extend feathery comblike appendages called cirri and feed on plankton. Here, the barnacles' cirri are in various states of retraction and extension. Goose barnacles often attach themselves to free-floating logs, bottles, or other flotsam.
Nakwakto Rapids, British Columbia. F. Stuart Westmorland.

intertidal wanderer an enchanting glimpse of underwater life. In these pools there is hardly ever any rough-and-tumble, and the animals that live within them have a continuous supply of moisture. As a result, animals do not shut their shells or hide under seaweed fronds. An observer can watch barnacles straining water for food, crabs scampering, and anemones blooming, instead of being sucked inward to prevent drying out.

Intertidal communities tend to be crowded; space is at a premium. If such densely packed habitats were left in relative quiet, a few long-term dominants would inevitably push out other less competitive species. But physical disruption—surf, storms, drift logs beating against the shore, winter ice, and the like—buffets the intertidal community. Ultimately, this leads to a greater diversity of species.

above: *Blue mussels, barnacles, periwinkle snails, and red encrusting algae in intertidal area. The organisms in this area compete intensely for space. The periwinkles, for instance, graze upon the red algae and slowly chip away at the rocks, causing the pool to enlarge over time.*
Appledore Island, Maine. Thomas Wiewandt.

right: *Intertidal organisms are often exposed to air at low tide and submerged at high tide. When the tide ebbs, they must conserve fluid, take shelter under seaweeds, or find pools of water.*
Pacific Northwest. Nancy Sefton.

Generally speaking, natural disturbances, which tend to be local and temporary, contribute to the overall health of rocky coastal habitats; they enhance biological diversity. Disturbances caused by human activities, such as pollution and physical alteration of a coastal habitat, are more permanent and pervasive than the natural kind, and usually reduce the diversity of species.

ESTUARIES AND WETLANDS

The chief physical characteristic of estuaries is the interplay of fresh water flowing in from the land with tidal salt water flowing in from the sea. Salt water is significantly denser than fresh water, and in most estuaries the fresh water lies over the salt water. In one typical configuration, known as a salt-wedge estuary, tidal salt water flows inward along the bottom, varying its reach with the tidal cycle, while above this salt wedge a layer of fresh water flows outward toward the ocean. If an estuary is sufficiently exposed, winds may reduce stratification by mixing the waters from top to bottom.

Species diversity varies considerably from one estuary to another. When they are not polluted, estuaries are highly productive, and they provide much of the seafood consumed by humans. Healthy estuaries are also nursery areas; both resident species and species from ocean waters beyond the estuary lay their eggs and spend their youth—their larval and juvenile stages—within these waters. When they reach maturity, the ocean dwellers move back to sea. Migratory shorebirds rely heavily upon estuaries as feeding and breeding grounds. If these visitors are included, the species diversity of an estuary becomes considerably larger than it appears to be at first glance.

Wetlands lie along the fringes of most estuaries. In temperate regions, these generally take the form of salt marshes; in tropical regions they are mangrove swamps. Both regions feature submerged sea grass beds.

To help solve the problems associated with waterlogged roots and to help support their leafy crowns, mangroves grow prop roots that descend directly from their branches into the water. Mangroves thus create a unique habitat as their roots and prop roots spread out over the bottom. Numerous animals attach themselves to the underwater portions of the prop roots, and the structural framework also provides protected nursery spaces where the young of many offshore species live through their early life stages.
Bahamas. Alex Kirkbride.

Salt marshes are dominated by grasses and sedges. These are home to many bird species and a number of coastal mammals. Numerous algae, small fish, and invertebrates thrive in the drainage channels that cut across the grassy flats.

With their great prop roots resembling flying buttresses, and their curving crowns thrust into the sky like vaulting arches, mangrove trees form natural cathedrals within tropical wetlands. While the trees themselves may support a number of avian, reptilian, and mammalian species, the truly estuarine species are to be found among the roots. The mangroves provide a protected environment for numerous juvenile fish, including some species common to coral reefs on the fringe of coastal swamps. A variety of invertebrates, such as shrimp, also inhabit the waters around the mangrove roots.

The submerged beds of sea grass found in shallow estuaries and lagoons are dominated by plant species from land that have readapted to water. In temperate regions the dominant submerged flowering plant is called eelgrass, while a different but related species, known as turtle grass, dominates

above: *The great white heron is a subspecies of the great blue heron. Herons' long bills are ideally suited for snatching prey out of the water. They patiently search for food—small animals swimming in the water—as they stand for hours on end. Everglades National Park, Florida. Frank Balthis.*

right: *Manatees live in fresh water and coastal marine water, where they feed on the sea grasses and other aquatic vegetation. Since they feed on submerged vegetation that requires light, the Atlantic Ocean manatees and their Pacific and Indian Ocean counterparts, the dugongs, never leave shallow coastal waters unless driven offshore by hazardous conditions. For instance, the oil spills in the Persian Gulf during the Gulf War in 1991 caused dugongs to flee to deeper water. Florida West Coast. Doug Perrine.*

above: *Fiddler crabs are among the most common animals found on the mud flats and sand flats of intertidal coastal lands. The fiddler crab digs a burrow home above the high-tide line for protection from the elements. The large claw, which only males have, is used to intimidate males and also as a noisemaker in courtship. The sound of a crab pounding the ground with its claw can be heard by females up to 30 feet away.*
Cape May County, New Jersey. Michael Baytoff.

left: *These reeds are in the freshwater portion of the Everglades. Emergent plants, those with underwater roots and above-water leaves, play an important role in wetland environments. Often the underwater portions of their stalks provide habitats for animals. Salt marshes, the main coastal wetlands of temperate regions, are dominated by emergent plants such as cordgrasses.*
Everglades, Florida. Michael Baytoff.

tropical sea grass beds. As the names of the grasses indicate, eels are common in the temperate estuaries, and sea turtles, particularly when they come shoreward to lay eggs, frequent the waters where turtle grass grows. Manatees and dugongs (sea cows) are also common in tropical sea grass beds, and actually graze on the plants. Numerous fish species, especially juvenile stages of estuarine and ocean species, live among the stalks. In fact, submerged sea grass beds, whether in temperate or tropical regions, serve a crucial role as fish nursery areas.

GIANT KELP BEDS

A much greater variety of seaweeds can be found along rocky coasts than in deeper, offshore waters. But one very remarkable type of seaweed-dominated community can be found offshore in waters 50 to 100 feet deep.

Giant kelp, a single species of brown seaweed, lives near the west coasts of parts of North and South America and in a few other continental-shelf locations. Anchored by holdfasts in the rocky shelf sediments, the kelp plants send sturdy, flexible stalks, up to 300 feet long, toward the surface. The stalks then sport leafy fronds held aloft by gas-filled balls, allowing the kelp to carry out photosynthesis where the sunlight is strongest.

Giant kelp forests provide a habitat for a diverse community of animals. Sea urchins graze on the kelp, and abalone and other shellfish dwell in these forests. Here, too, is the domain of the lovable and clever sea otter, a key predator that feeds on the sea urchin and thus helps the kelp to flourish.

Sea otters are among the few tool-using animals. If you visit a kelp forest, you might find an otter floating on its back on the surface with a stone balanced on its stomach. In the otter's paws will be an urchin or perhaps a shellfish, which the otter will be opening by striking it against the stone.

For a time, fur traders in California and others whose livelihood depended on shellfish killed off great numbers of sea otters in order to increase profits. The idea backfired. Without otters to eat the sea urchins, the urchins proliferated and ate the kelp, denuding the forest and ultimately reducing the shellfish population. People have now discovered the importance of sea otters, and there is a movement to protect them. In certain areas, however, the otters have never come back and the kelp forests have never recovered.

right: *Garibaldi in kelp forest. California. Howard Hall.*

overleaf: *Sea otter and baby. Hawaii. James D. Watt.*

CORAL REEFS

Tropical coral reefs are the best-known and most-photographed underwater communities. Warm temperatures, luminous waters, and the remarkable colors and shapes of a seemingly endless diversity of plants, fishes, and invertebrates attract legions of snorkelers, scuba divers, fishermen, and underwater photographers. Indeed, coral reefs have the highest species diversity of any marine biome now known.

The reefs generally are long strips of coral deposits running parallel to a coastline. They fall into three categories: barrier reefs, atolls, and fringing reefs. A barrier reef is an irregular stretch of coastal coral linked with islands, subtidal reefs, and lagoons. The largest and most famous of these is the Great Barrier Reef off the northeast coast of Australia. An atoll is a deposit of coral that is circular or horseshoe-shaped. Sometimes these deposits rise a few feet out of the water, creating an island that surrounds a central lagoon. A fringing reef is a smaller deposit of coral, usually very close to shore and too small to form an island or lagoon.

Different species of coral form different characteristic shapes, which are usually adaptations to wave action. Smooth shapes, such as those of the brain coral, are more resistant to wave motion, and are common in the shallower depths of the reef. Branching forms, such as the staghorn coral, survive better at deeper levels, out of reach of wave action.

Coral reefs are justly celebrated for their marvelous diversity of animal life. This diversity tends to increase with depth, down to the level where lack of light limits the growth of corals. There is also a distinct global pattern: the reefs that are home to the greatest varieties of animal life occur in the western Pacific, while species diversity decreases the farther

Lionfish over coral reef. The lionfish is one of the many venomous animals living on a coral reef, and its poisonous fin spines make it unpalatable and dangerous to many predators, including humans. Red Sea. Chris Newbert.

Nudibranch. The word nudibranch means "exposed gills," and these beautiful animals are also known as sea slugs, because they are marine snails without shells. Nudibranch species come in a variety of brilliant colors. The coloration can either act as camouflage on a bright coral reef or as a vivid warning to predators to keep their distance from a potentially distasteful meal. Vanuatu. Brian Ansell.

east one goes. The same pattern holds true in the Atlantic.

Many kinds of seaweed make their homes in reefs, but these are usually kept closely cropped by reef herbivores. In fact, a noteworthy seaweed crop is usually a sign of an unhealthy reef. Increased standing crops of seaweed shade the corals and reduce the photosynthetic efficiency of the zooxanthellae, the microscopic algae that have been incorporated into coral tissue. Seaweed crop increases can be the result of increased nutrient loads or of the disappearance of a sufficient population of grazers. Both often reflect undue interference by humans.

Reefs support a high diversity of animals because they provide a complex and variable physical structure, increasing the variety of available habitats, both large and small. The fact that reefs are found in tropical waters in itself increases the potential diversity found there, since species diversity tends to increase as one approaches the equator. And in reefs, as in rocky shore communities, diversity is enhanced by intermittent physical disturbances, predation, and competition.

Red soft coral belongs to the same phylum as jellyfish, anemones, hard corals, gorgonians, and sea pens. In soft corals, the polyps are united into a colony by a soft, flexible matrix or core. Gorgonians, on the other hand, have a core made of hard, horny material. Red Sea. Amos Nachoum.

Star coral is one of about 1,000 species of hard, or stony, coral. Other species form a variety of shapes, including elkhorn, brain, lettuce, and plate corals—each named according to its formation. The more solid corals that live in shallow waters have adapted to the significant wave action; the more fragile, branched forms grow in deeper waters and are protected from waves. Solomon Islands. Burt Jones & Maurine Shimlock.

The mushroom coral is unusual among hard coral because it can move as an adult. Although corals are mobile as larvae, they typically settle on the bottom and remain sedentary in their adult stage. The mushroom coral uses tentacles to move. Fiji. Burt Jones & Maurine Shimlock.

overleaf: *Blue-green chromis over staghorn coral. Great Barrier Reef, Australia. Fred Bavendam.*

To those who have seen them, coral reefs are probably the most beautiful of ocean habitats. They are also one of the most fragile; ironically, this is the habitat most threatened by the activities of humans.

Coral polyps can live only at depths where light is sufficient to support photosynthesis—about 50 feet maximum. As sea levels change—the sea is now rising—the coral reefs can usually keep pace by depositing layer upon layer of calcium carbonate year after year. But they can do so only if sea levels do not change at a rate faster than the coral can grow. The accelerated pace of sea-level rise caused by global warming (caused by human behavior) poses a stark threat to the survival of coral reefs worldwide. Corals may sink below the maximum depths at which they can photosynthesize efficiently.

The rising temperature in some of the equatorial regions of the sea poses another threat to the corals' existence. Corals can thrive only within a very narrow temperature range, and the upper limit of

right: *Anemone fish in anemone. Anemone fish can mate for life, and sometimes the same pair will live in an anemone for years. Typically, they lay their eggs around the base of the anemone. Fiji. David Hall.*

below: *Anemone mouth. Anemones are closely related to hard corals, but unlike the filter-feeding hard corals, anemones grasp and devour prey as large as small fish. Anemones are common to coral reefs and in almost all other marine environments, including intertidal and deep-sea ecosystems. Monterey Bay, California. Norbert Wu.*

Banded shrimp on coral. Like a candy-striped volunteer, the banded coral shrimp, or peppermint shrimp, may use its red and white color bands to indicate that it is available to clean fish. The coral head this shrimp is standing on may be a marker that indicates to fish that this is a cleaning station.
Caribbean. Scott Frier.

that range is being surpassed during the warmest times of year. These periods of temperature stress are associated with a phenomenon called bleaching—the corals turn white—caused by the sudden release of zooxanthellae from the corals. Global warming, caused by air pollution, appears to be behind the temperature increases.

Water pollution can also harm reefs. Since the life of the coral reef depends upon clear waters, soil and fertilizers running off the land can create havoc in the community. First, sediments may smother the reef and cut out the light. Then nutrients stimulate the phytoplankton. The excess microalgae die and decompose; this reduces oxygen in the water, and also clouds the water so that essential sunlight does not reach the deeper corals.

Finally, there are the threats posed by such seemingly harmless activities as snorkeling and scuba diving. Some divers do not realize that standing on or even brushing against fragile corals may, over time, damage and deplete reef communities. And, of

course, collecting corals eventually results in an absence of corals to collect. Other seemingly innocuous behaviors can be damaging—the use of sun-protection lotions by swimmers, for example. The lotions harm reef communities, especially those visited by large numbers of tourists, like the reefs off Cozumel, Mexico.

People fishing for food or collecting reef animals for sale to the aquarium trade can deplete populations of fish and invertebrates. Blasting coral reefs with explosives as a quick means of catching loads of fish has destroyed reefs off the Philippines and elsewhere. Aquarium harvesting is most often accomplished by spreading low doses of cyanide over an area of reef. Many fish die in the process, while others are merely stunned; the stunned fish are then collected, but most of these die in transport. Only a few of the fish removed from the reef actually find their way into aquarium tanks. The educational, aesthetic, and *economic* value hardly makes up for the destruction and loss.

Like their relatives the squid and octopus, cuttlefish are able to change color rapidly and may be bioluminescent. The cuttlefish's internal shell, the cuttlebone, often washes ashore, and humans have found a variety of uses for it. The cuttlebone can be used by bird keepers to provide calcium and beak sharpeners for pet birds. Cuttlebone can be used to sharpen knives, and it formerly even had medicinal applications.
Lizard Island, Great Barrier Reef, Australia. Fred Bavendam.

above: *Fish on dynamited reef. Dynamite-fishing techniques have laid waste to the coral reefs of the Philippines and other tropical Pacific Islands. The entire reef ecosystem is destroyed, and recovery takes many years if it happens at all. Philippines. Lynn Funkhouser.*

right: *Longnose filefish feed exclusively on the polyps of Acopora corals and are found in calm waters wherever this coral abounds. The filefish uses its long, pointed snout to pluck the polyps from their cuplike skeletons. This delicate feeding behavior differs from that of the triggerfish and parrot fish, which bite off and grind up chunks of hard coral to reach the fleshy polyps inside. Fiji. David Hall.*

overleaf: *Arrow crabs. San Salvador, Bahamas. Brian Ansell.*

OCEANIC ECOSYSTEMS

The open ocean is an environment in motion. The diverse species in this environment therefore move about by drifting, by their own locomotion through the water, or by a combination of both.

Many of the planktonic animals make daily vertical excursions, traveling upward toward the surface at night and downward to the depths in the daytime. Some journey 600 to 900 feet or more. Some species of nearly every major group of animals found in the plankton—crustaceans, protozoa, jellyfish, worms, tunicates, young fish, and several others—have evolved this behavior.

Deep-sea plankton and numerous small deep-sea fish also exhibit dramatic vertical migrations. These patterns were first noticed when echo-sounding measurements designed to map the sea bottom picked up a sound-reflecting layer at mid-ocean depths. Widespread sonar measurements have confirmed the existence of the layer (known as the deep scattering layer) in all oceans except the polar seas.

The animals that swim through the ocean, the nekton, travel from one place to another or from one depth to another under their own power; they are directed by their own whims or inner drives rather than by the dominant movement of the ocean currents. Most of these animals are vertebrates, including the large schooling fish such as tuna and perch, sharks and rays, swordfish and sailfish, and many marine mammals. All of them move through the water by virtue of muscular action, with the fins providing balance, direction, and speed. The tail fin is the main propeller; almost all fish also have median fins along the back and underside of the tail. The inner ear is used to maintain equilibrium and to sense

Mating sea butterflies. These beautiful animals are pteropod mollusks, pelagic sea snails without shells. Unlike most mollusks, which creep about on surfaces, these graceful animals float among the plankton in the surface waters of the open ocean. York, Maine. Fred Bavendam.

change of direction. The ears and special external organs called lateral line organs are sensitive to nearby disturbances in the water; these help to detect and locate prey as well as mates and to avoid obstacles.

Marine mammals are efficient swimmers, gracefully gliding through the water with seemingly little effort. Because they breathe air and must return to the surface frequently to take a breath, speed is important. To hold one's breath for an hour or more seems to us a very long time, but a whale diving to great depths in its search for food has much to accomplish between breaths. Speed and efficiency of motion are critical.

In contrast to fish, which propel themselves by a sideways movement of the tail fin, whales and dolphins propel themselves through the water primarily by an upward stroke of their powerful tails. The tail fins of whales, accordingly, are oriented in a horizontal plane, while those of fish are vertical. Most whales and dolphins also have a distinct fin, the dorsal fin, rising from the back. This stabilizes

the animal, and is apparently also used to regulate temperature. The front flippers are used for steering.

Diving to great depths for as long as an hour or more presents challenges to the breathing mechanisms of marine mammals. Humans with air tanks risk serious trouble if they dive deep and then return to the surface too rapidly. Under the increased pressures at depth, nitrogen—a normal component of the air—dissolves in the blood. As a diver ascends and the surrounding pressure drops, some of the dissolved nitrogen comes out of solution again. If the ascent is too rapid, the nitrogen bubbles collect in the diver's body at points other than the lungs, causing a condition called the bends, which can be fatal.

Deep-diving whales avoid these problems by chemically storing a large supply of oxygen in their

The difference between cetacean and fish tails is shown here. The whales at right are cetaceans and have broad, horizontally flat tails that move up and down. The sailfish above has a vertically flat tail, which it swings from side to side. Sailfish roam the expanses of the open ocean and have been recorded swimming as fast as 70 miles an hour.
above: *Venezuela. Doug Perrine.*

left: *Alaska. James Gritz.*

muscles, so that they can maintain movement for long periods of time without fresh air. At depth, the air in their lungs is forced into the windpipe, where it is essentially sealed off and prevented from entering the bloodstream. When the whale surfaces, it explosively expels used air accumulated during the dive, producing a spout of spray rising from the dorsal blowhole. The whale then inhales, expanding fully the air sacs of the lungs in order to absorb fresh gases rapidly into the blood. When these gases are fully absorbed, the whale is ready to dive again.

Whales have a very highly developed sense of hearing, and they can communicate with each other by means of a number of different sounds. Some baleen whales use low-frequency sounds to communicate over distances of hundreds of miles by using sound channels in the ocean. The toothed whales track their prey using echolocation. They emit short,

above: *The massive blue whale is the largest animal ever to roam the Earth. At birth a blue whale is 23 feet long and weighs 5,500 pounds. It grows at a rate of 8 pounds per hour (200 pounds a day), ultimately reaching a length of more than 100 feet and a weight of up to 150 tons, and its heart alone weighs several tons. Blue whales, which roam the Atlantic and Pacific Oceans in both the Northern and Southern hemispheres, were terribly exploited during the first half of this century, and the original population of 200,000 was nearly decimated when the whalers moved into fertile Antarctic waters. When commercial whaling of blue whales was banned in the Southern Hemisphere in 1965, there were about 6,000 blue whales remaining in the world. California. Mark Conlin.*

right: *Manta rays, weighing up to 3,000 pounds, usually move languidly through the water, gracefully flapping their giant wings. Periodically, however, they generate enough power to lift their bodies entirely clear of the water, perhaps to dislodge parasites. Cocos Island, Costa Rica. F. Stuart Westmorland.*

Whale shark and golden trevally fish. The fish in the school of golden trevally in the foreground need not worry about being eaten by the whale shark lurking behind them. The whale shark, which grows up to 50 feet and 40,000 pounds and is the largest fish in the ocean, eats nothing larger than tiny fish and plankton strained out of the water. Whale sharks sometimes feed by placing their bodies upright in the water with their mouths facing up and bobbing up and down near the surface. The imposing mouth can be 6 to 10 feet wide and contain as many as 5,000 tiny teeth. Sea of Cortez. Howard Hall.

intense pulses of ultrasonic sounds (sound waves of shorter length than humans can hear). These bounce off objects and produce a sonic map of the whale's surroundings.

Marine mammals have thick layers of blubber under the skin to help keep them warm. Blubber has another function: it undulates as the animal swims, enhancing the forward movement of the animal. Dolphins can swim at over 35 miles per hour, partly because they are very strong, partly because their skin surface adjusts shape to reduce drag.

Squids use jet propulsion, and the short-distance speed they can reach is probably faster than that of any other species in the open ocean. Squid are seldom caught in nets: they are able to react quickly and avoid them. Some species, known as flying squid, even jump out of the water to avoid danger.

Squid vary in size from several inches to 50 feet in length, and are so shy, so wary, and so quick that much of our information about their diversity and abundance comes to us indirectly—from the

Krill. A blue whale feeds almost solely on krill and can eat almost 5 tons a day when it is in the Antarctic. Krill are also a mainstay food for fin, sei, minke, and humpback whales.
Pacific Ocean off Baja, California. Frank Balthis.

guts of predators who have eaten them. Indeed, giant squid, who live mostly in the deep ocean, have only rarely been seen by humans. Giant squid are a favored food of the toothed sperm whale, but they are not an easy meal. Many sperm whales bear permanent sucker scars that attest to the struggle the great squids have put up before being devoured.

above: *Bottlenose dolphins are found in open water and in bays, estuaries, and other enclosed areas. They are social animals and often gather in pods. These are the dolphins one usually sees in aquarium shows. A bottlenose dolphin's brain actually weighs more than that of a human.*
Baja, California. Kevin Schafer.

left: *Although it is much larger than most plankton, the jellyfish is considered a type of plankton because it has limited mobility. It can slowly move by undulating its bell but is largely at the mercy of prevailing currents.*
Coronado Island, California. Norbert Wu.

POLAR SEAS

The Arctic Ocean and the Southern Ocean surrounding Antarctica are special oceanic environments because of the presence of ice on the surface. Polar waters are cold, but they are incredibly rich in nutrients, which means a prolific production of food during the season when there is enough light to drive high rates of photosynthesis.

Although ice interferes with light penetration into the waters below, some microalgae have adapted to this limitation by living within the ice, or on its underside. Some bacteria, protozoa, and planktonic crustaceans, including krill, shrimplike animals about two to four inches long, do so also. While in the ice itself, they are eaten only by animals that can scrape the lower ice or can take chunks out of it.

When the ice melts in the summer, the plankton released into the water begin a period of rapid reproduction. Algal populations bloom, feeding animals from the surface to the bottom depths. The animal populations also explode.

Meanwhile, in both polar locations, filter-feeding whales take advantage of the blooms. Whales migrating to the Arctic feed on the small animals in the bottom sediments, while whales migrating to the Southern Ocean find vast blooms of krill to feast upon in the surface waters.

Diversity in the Arctic and Antarctic environments is further enhanced by a system of open traces and holes where ice has been driven away by winds and where relatively warm water rises from the ocean beneath, bringing with it a rich supply of nutrients. Thanks to the ample sunlight of summer, food productivity in these areas is high, and therefore they are hospitable environments for seabirds and

The adult penguin has no enemies on land and can generally outrace its predators at sea, but is vulnerable when it first jumps into the water. Leopard seals, killer whales, and sea lions often lie waiting in ambush in the dangerous waters below.
Palmer Peninsula, Antarctic. Flip Nicklin.

overleaf: *Polar bears. Arctic. Flip Nicklin.*

mammals. Many of these "summer resorts" are created in the same locations every year. Naturally, hungry animals know to look for them.

Because polar seas are greatly threatened by pollution and overfishing, the Antarctic Treaty of 1990 will make a very important permanent difference to the Southern Ocean. According to the terms of the treaty, exploitation of minerals is prohibited, and the continent is to be a totally protected wilderness, with only scientific research and regulated tourism allowed. The surrounding ocean also receives special protection from shipping, whaling, and all sources of pollution.

The Arctic is not so fortunate. Overfishing, oil pollution, industrial pollution, and radioactive waste disposal all threaten this important but fragile ecosystem. The effects of global warming are expected to be felt in the northern polar latitudes more than elsewhere.

The actual warming of the ocean water is not the gravest threat to the Arctic Ocean ecosystem, for

above: *All animals in polar areas are exposed to cold, but babies are most vulnerable. The young harp seal has a different color coat from its mother, and this is, in part, an adaptation to the cold. The hair appears white but is actually translucent, enabling the baby's skin to absorb the warmth of the sun. The pure white coat also provides camouflage as it enables the baby to blend in against a snowy background. The fur is valuable to some people for purposes of fashion, and harp seal babies are slaughtered in droves. Labrador, Canada. Scott Frier.*

left: *Krill under ice. Though krill is a name given by Norwegian whalers to refer to a specific species of plankton found only in the Antarctic, the term is also used to refer generically to many other shrimplike, planktonic animals found throughout the ocean. Krill grow no longer than 3 inches, but they occur in massive numbers. Palmer Peninsula, Antarctic. Flip Nicklin.*

most species could survive that warming, and perhaps would even enjoy it. The problem is that the ice would melt, along with the tundra permafrost. This melting would destroy the special ice habitat critical to many species and introduce large amounts of fresh water into the Arctic Ocean, which could alter the worldwide system of ocean currents.

HYDROTHERMAL VENTS, SUBMARINE CANYONS, AND TRENCHES

The greatest depths of the ocean floor are found at the bottoms of submarine canyons and trenches. The Mariana Trench, the deepest on Earth, reaches a depth of nearly seven miles below sea level. Deep canyons similarly cut across the high slopes of the seafloor.

The side walls of trenches and canyons are subject to crumbling and are scoured by strong currents. Meanwhile, the bottoms receive a continual supply of sediment and debris from the crumbling walls and from the plains above. All of this physical activity creates an environment that is much too unstable to support a high diversity of benthic species, but it may be home to tenacious wall-clingers and deep-water pelagic animals. Some canyons, such as the Monterey Canyon off the coast of California, are considered scientific treasure chests of unusual fauna.

Hydrothermal vents occur along the geologically active plate margins and central mountain ridges of the ocean floor. These vent communities are small areas, the size of football fields, where warm water, gases, and minerals, some of which are highly toxic, seep out of Earth's crust. Because they are small and remote, hydrothermal vents were not discovered by scientists until the 1970s, when submersible vessels began to be used to explore the deep-sea bottom.

The first photos and television pictures of vent communities revealed a world of exceeding strangeness. Weird, surprisingly large animals were found thriving where it was thought no living creatures could possibly exist: this is an environment

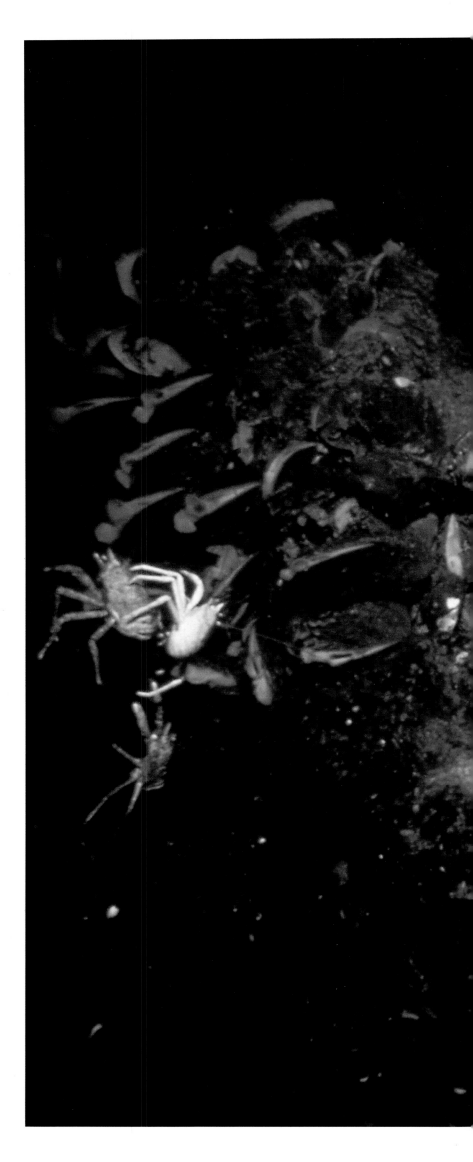

Mussels, clams, and galatheid crab in deep-sea vent community. The vent community environments are anaerobic (lacking oxygen) and are rich in materials such as sulfides, petroleum hydrocarbons, and heavy metals that are toxic to ordinary organisms. Galápagos. Robert Hessler.

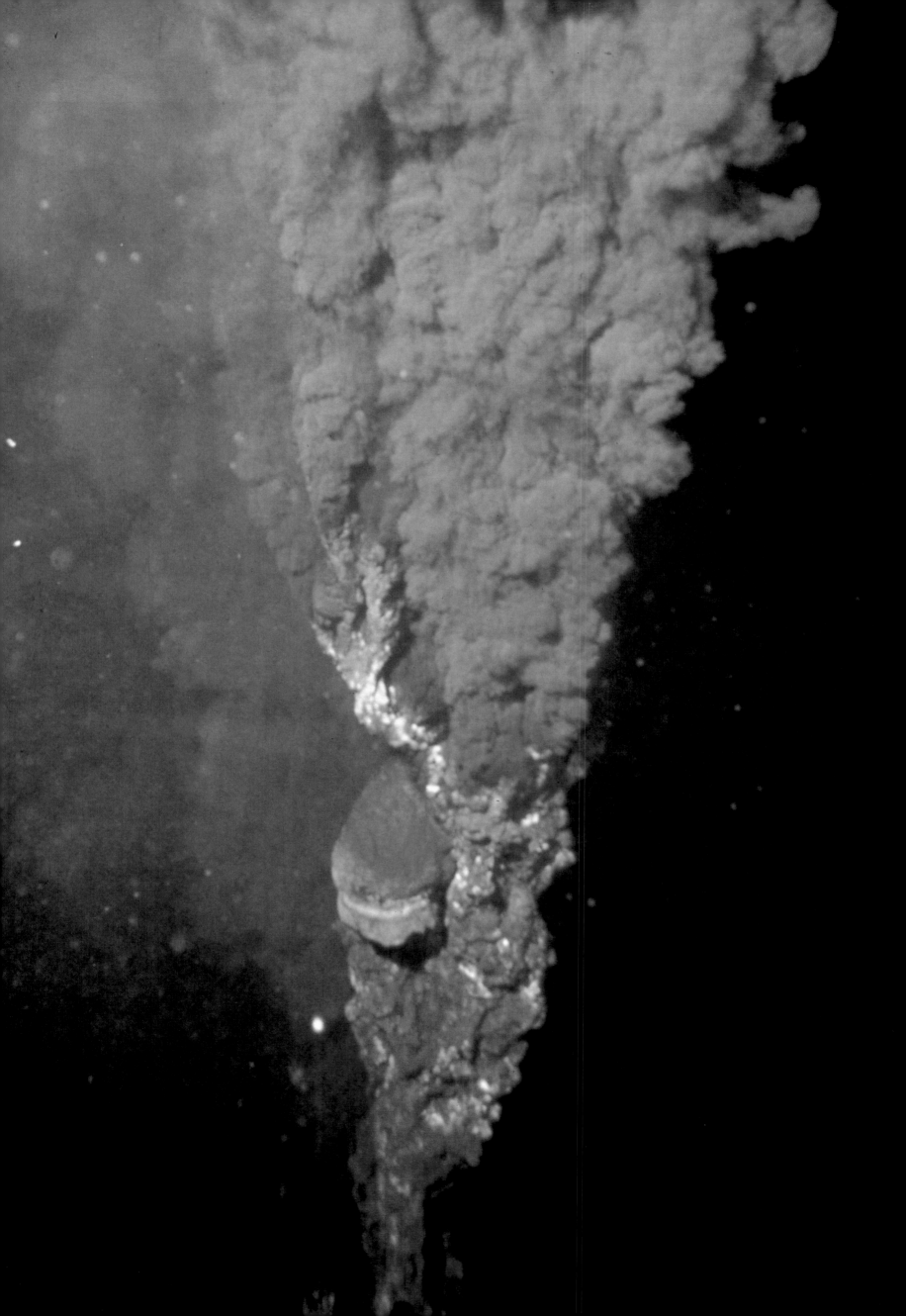

where there is no oxygen, where ambient temperatures are close to boiling, and where there are high concentrations of potentially toxic materials, such as sulfides, petroleum hydrocarbons, and heavy metals.

At the base of the vent food chain are chemosynthetic bacteria. These bacteria do not photosynthesize; instead, they use the energy of chemical bonds to transform simple nutrients into organic materials—living tissue. The bacteria fuel a community of animals that is relatively low in diversity, but unique to this environment: over a hundred species of invertebrates and fish have been identified so far. The best-known species is the giant tube worm, three to four feet in length.

Life—so fragile in the individual—is creative and resilient in the whole. Life always finds ways to spread her species and find them homes, in friendly environments, and even in environments that seem deadly.

above: *Tube worms have a symbiotic relationship with the bacteria that live within their bodies. Bacteria consume the hydrogen sulfide spewed forth from vents and synthesize sugars. The tube worms, which lack mouths and guts, consume the sugars produced by the bacteria. Tube worms are about three or four feet in length. Galápagos. Dudley Foster.*

left: *Black smoker. The hot water spewing from this vent is heated deep in the Earth near magma chambers and reaches temperatures of several hundred degrees Fahrenheit. The water is laced with hydrogen sulfide and other minerals. The chimney is formed when minerals dissolve out of the hot vent water, and can reach 150 feet in height. Undersea vents had been predicted by scientists in the 1960s but were not discovered until 1977, when the research submarine* Alvin *found them off the Galápagos. East Pacific Rise. Robert Ballard.*

overleaf: *Submersible. Grand Cayman. Courtney Platt.*

DEEP ABYSS

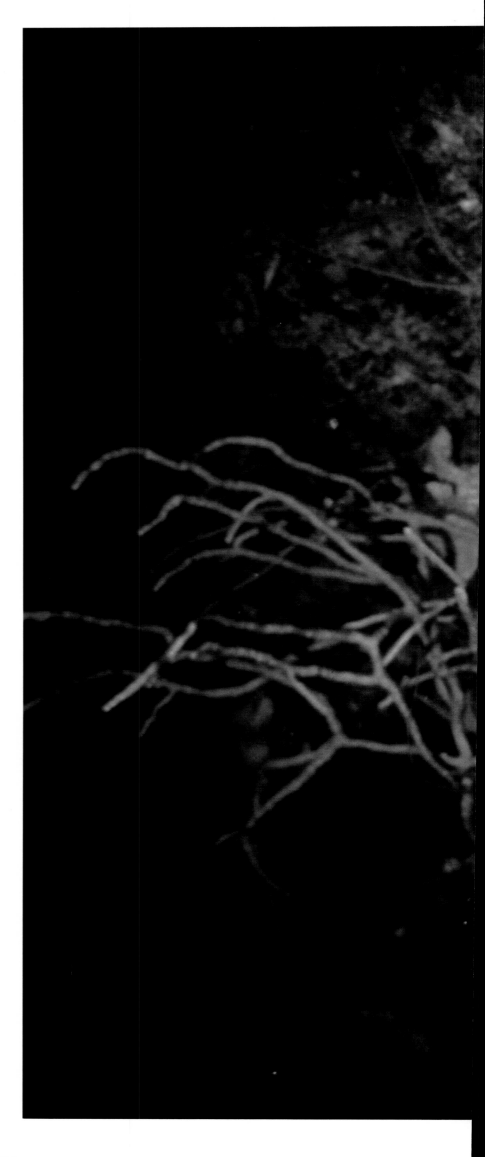

A submarine voyage across the ocean's deep abyssal regions reveals a seemingly lifeless, featureless plain—empty, cold, and utterly dark. In time, shapes begin to emerge: ranges of high mountains, some of them extending above the sea's surface (we know them as islands; the Azores, for instance); hotspots, where the heat of the planet's interior seeps out of the seafloor; deep submarine canyons; and even deeper and longer fissures called trenches which plunge four to seven miles down and stretch across the seafloor for hundreds of miles. But the most amazing feature of all is that the great undersea plain is teeming with life.

Hundreds of thousands, perhaps even millions, of species are spread out across the continental slopes and deep abyssal plains. Most are small, inconspicuous inhabitants of the organically rich sediments. How can an immense abundance of species live in such darkness and cold, and be subjected to such great pressure?

The abyss is a world without plants. Plants need light to live. Since animals do not photosynthesize, darkness is irrelevant to them. As long as there is light somewhere to fuel the production of organic material, some of this matter eventually finds its way into the deep ocean, where it becomes food. Small organic particles, bodies and feces of small plankton, rain down from the surface into the abyssal sediments. This rain is plentiful and constant, and it provides a predictable food supply for the bacteria and the detritus eaters that live down below. Of course, there is no available light to identify living prey or potential mates, but those species that need light produce it themselves—bioluminescence.

Tube sponge at 300 feet. This tube sponge is found in the deeper reaches of a coral reef, an area that receives little sunlight. Other sponges are found in even deeper areas of the ocean, such as trenches and canyons.
Grand Cayman. Courtney Platt.

Sea dandelions at 800 feet. Sea dandelions are soft corals and are related to jellyfish. Sea dandelions reproduce by budding off little planktonic medusoid individuals with eight tentacles. These disperse in the water and eventually settle to the bottom as polyps and produce colonies by budding.
Grand Cayman. Courtney Platt.

On the deep abyssal plain, temperatures are not too low to support life. On the contrary, the water that flows along the deep-ocean bottom originates in the Arctic, where it supports high biological production at the ocean surface. Predictably, the temperature of the deep ocean is relatively constant, and adapting to a constant low temperature is far easier than adapting to large temperature fluctuations. Biochemical processes will be somewhat slower in colder waters than elsewhere, but that simply defines the nature of life and by no means prevents it.

The immense pressure of the deep is also no barrier to the proliferation of life. Water is highly incompressible. Therefore, the pressure of a column of water two to seven miles high, awesome as that may seem, has relatively little effect either on the water itself or on the bodies of animals living in the abyss. In fact, generally speaking, the pressure within their bodies is roughly equivalent to the pressure outside. Those species living on the deep abyssal

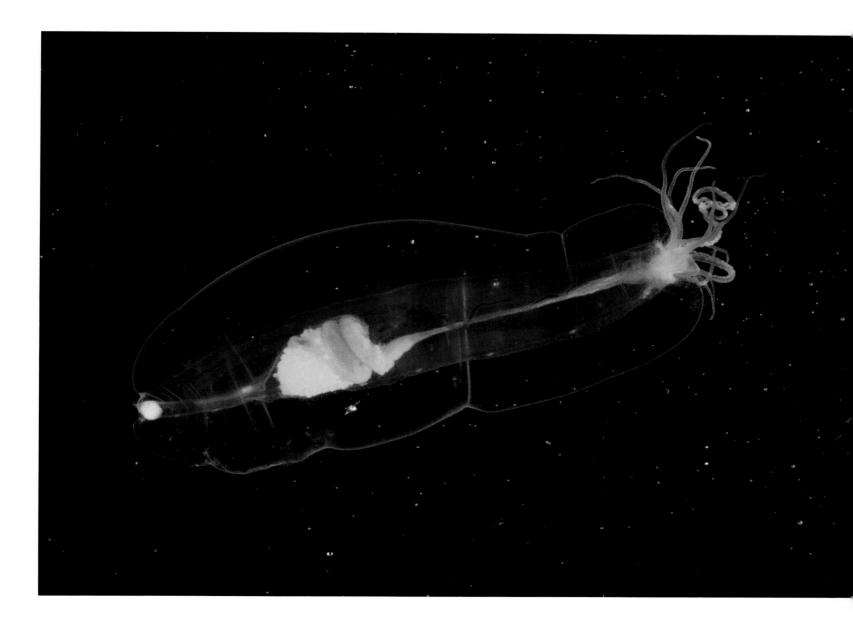

plain for the most part stay there. Those creatures that move around between depths have developed systems that allow them to do that safely.

To the human eye, the vast expanse of soft, even sediments across the abyssal plain appears featureless. The creatures dwelling within the sediments of the abyssal plain are very small, however, and encounter a variety of habitat that provides considerable differences in nutrition and structure. There is also a complexity on a larger scale that can be observed over time. As large pieces of organic debris—bodies of large oceanic animals or pieces of seaweed, for example—fall irregularly to the bottom, they provide a temporary habitat for organisms that also use them as a food source. Fish, crabs, and other animals can move from one such feeding ground to another.

This spatial and temporal diversity in food supply allows for the existence of a number of animal species that would not otherwise be supported by the

Worm. More than 80 percent of the ocean's water lies below 3,300 feet, far below the range of sunlight. The Monterey Canyon, located off Monterey Bay, California, is one of the most fertile areas for deep-sea research. This worm, suspended in the abyssal starlight of phosphorescence, is little more than a primitive stomach. Monterey Canyon. Sea Studios.

organic ooze in the sediment. And these species, in turn, are a food source for larger predatory animals, such as sharks, that frequent the deep abyss.

Two other factors probably contribute to the high species diversity of the deep-sea floor: first, the floor's great expanse (two-thirds of the Earth's surface), and, second, its freedom from large-scale catastrophic disturbances over long geological periods. To be sure, bottom currents or deep-sea storms may occasionally sweep over a particular area of the abyssal plain, but such temporary catastrophes probably encourage diversity, since they are almost certainly analogous to the effects of coastal storms on the rocky intertidal community. By clearing patches where new species may move in, storms serve to increase species diversity. It is a general rule of evolution that ecosystems characterized by a large area and by long periods without catastrophe have a high diversity of species: they provide more time and more space for new species to evolve.

Fangtooth. The fangtooth is a deep-sea aggressor. The adult fangtooth spends its entire life in the dark ocean depths and its development is affected by the demanding environment in which it lives. Fish of the deep tend to have small eyes, poorly developed muscles and skeletal systems, and metabolisms up to twenty times slower than those of fish of the upper ocean. California. Norbert Wu.

Cystosoma. A deep-sea planktonic animal, the cystosoma is an amphipod, related to sand fleas. Its enormous eyes are useful for low-light, deep-water life.
Laurence P. Madin.

overleaf: *Crested oarfish. Baja, California. Norbert Wu.*

The discovery that the ocean floor may support the greatest species diversity in the ocean, possibly even on Earth, astonished most ocean scientists, for it contradicted all their assumptions. Early deep-sea biologists reasoned that the high pressure, cold temperature, and scant food supply would support very few species. Even today a number of oceanographers, experts in the chemistry and physics of the deep ocean but not of the biology, persist in their claims that the abyss is a wasteland.

Nothing could be further from the truth, and it is essential to dispel such myths before we make terrible mistakes in deciding how to treat the deep-ocean environment. There are people who advocate using the ocean floor as a massive dumping ground for all the poisonous refuse of our industrial societies—the "out of sight, out of mind" thinking that has already caused so much environmental damage. On the other hand, many other people recognize the biological wealth of the deep ocean and advocate protecting the ecosystem as a wilderness—a wilderness deserving protection for its value to scientific research and its importance to the biological heritage of this planet now and in the future.

In the nurturing environment of the ocean, life arose and spread and diversified, to fill the multiplicity of niches and habitats to be found in the immense depths and stretches of an interconnected body of water. Over time, most of the forms life has taken have been lost, but the ocean is still the cradle of life, and the repository of most of the genetic information on Earth. And the ocean is still filled with living splendor, from microscopic phytoplankton all the way through to gigantic, gentle whales. May we do all we can to keep it that way.

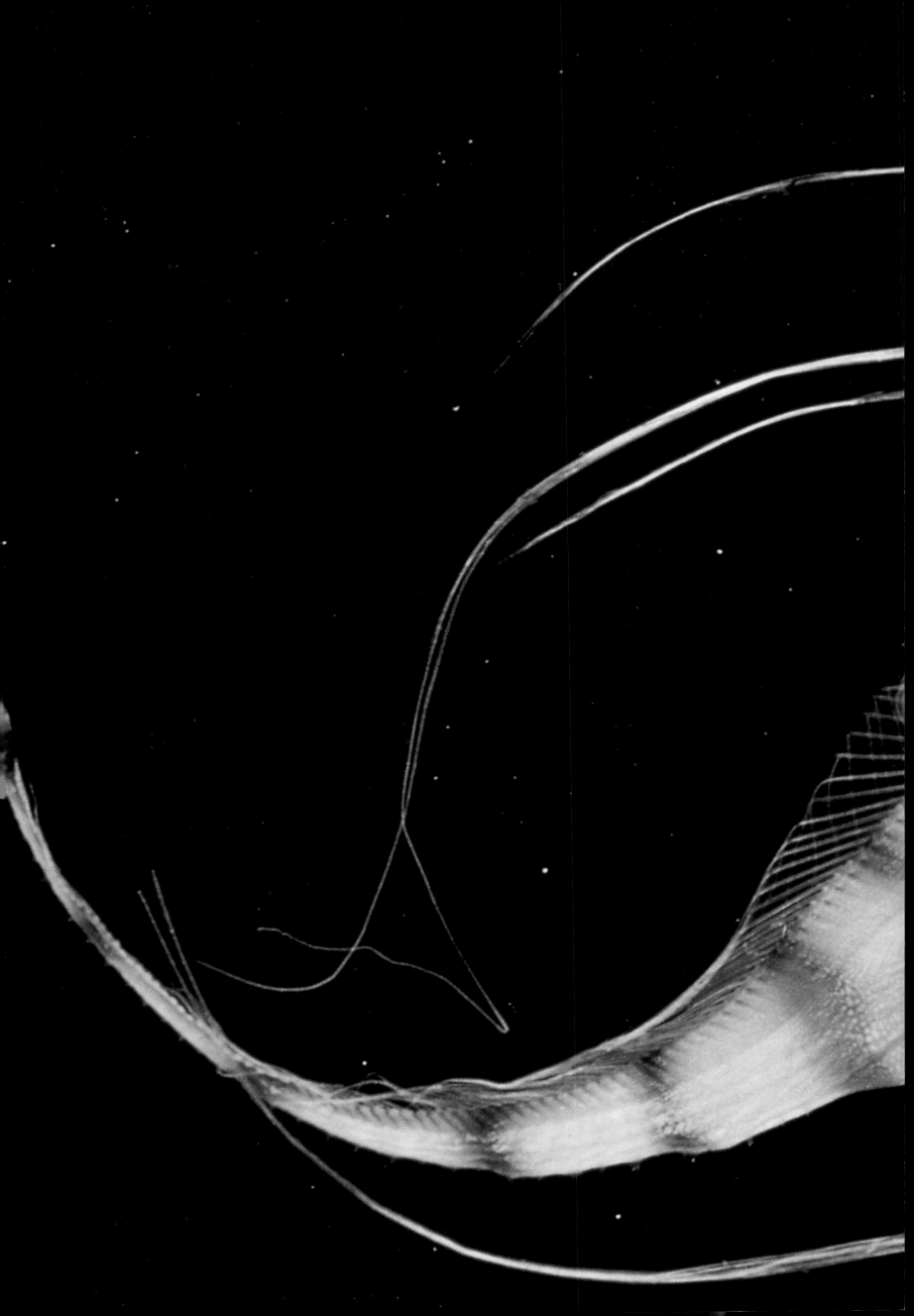

SCOTT FRIER
Nikon Underwater Technical Expert
Former Chief Expedition Photographer for the Cousteau Society

I am a fan of the little guys in the ocean, the many small plants and animals that give the seas their incredible richness and beauty. Perhaps because these little guys are not big and dramatic, or pretty and cuddly, people don't often appreciate them and see their importance in the ecosystem and their struggles for survival. The little guys deserve attention, too, just like the whales.

It took several years of diving for me to appreciate the incredible beauty and variety in the ocean. My education began when I got serious about underwater photography and realized that there were very few dives where you could see giant sharks, but that with every dive there was a lot of beauty in the common inhabitants of the sea.

For example, there's a small fish off Fiji called the Ewa blenny. The blennies are not much larger than your finger, and they live in the abandoned holes of tubeworms. I approached one once while it was swimming in front of its hole and stuck my glove in the entrance of its tiny hole. The fish just looked at my glove, and you could see the look of shock on its face. It became angry,

Ewa blenny. Fiji.
Scott Frier.

and it swam around in a panic attack trying to pull the glove out with its mouth. It got very frustrated until I pulled the glove out. It came back and saw the glove was gone. You could see the fish stop in his tracks, practically go "Oh my god," and then dart back in his hole. It was so relieved. I love that kind of interaction with the ocean's "little guys."

I try to pass this appreciation on when I teach underwater photography. I encourage my students to look creatively at the small stuff; to try to take the usual and make it unusual. Everybody wants to photograph sharks and whales, but the truth is that most people will see very few, if any, of them during a diving career. Whenever

Ewa blenny. This small fish became agitated when Scott Frier stuck his diving glove into its hole.
Fiji. Scott Frier.

I give a presentation of my photographs. I try to stay away from the big stuff that people know about or see frequently; I try to concentrate on the little guy. I want to popularize the ordinary by demonstrating the enormous beauty that can be captured with a little creativity and patience.

I never eat anything from the sea. It's not a moral thing. They're my pals. These fish are like puppies. Sometimes I watch them for hours as I wait for the right moment to take the photograph. I learn about their lives, their behaviors, their problems. Over the years I have developed a respect for their lives.

Captain Cousteau says that people protect what they love. If more people could see what a treasure of life we have in the sea, there would be more of a hue and cry over the damage we are doing to this underwater world. But people have difficulty conceiving what is for them a mysterious, hidden undersea world.

No matter how much you look at photographs of the Grand Canyon, there's no way to understand its grandeur and immensity until you've actually been there and looked over the edge or hiked to the bottom. It's the same with a coral reef or a kelp forest. The problem is the comparatively small number of people who have actually seen a coral reef firsthand. Probably more people get a chance to appreciate the Grand Canyon in one year than have ever had the chance to enjoy the biodiversity of a coral reef or kelp forest.

Regardless of how often I've done it, and I've been diving thousands of times, when I'm swimming through a kelp forest on a sunny California afternoon with the light streaming down through the kelp and seals swimming by, it's like walking—or even flying—through a sun-splashed underwater forest. Sometimes I just have to put down my camera, sit back, and say, "Holy smokes, we live in a beautiful world."

SAMUEL LaBUDDE
Biologist

In groping for a succinct and compelling argument to use against the purse-seining of dolphins and the use of high seas driftnets, activities that have no place in humanity's responsible stewardship of the planet, it dawned on me that dolphins represent the only species on Earth that value human life. So much for the succinct part; the compelling part came in trying to understand why.

If you anesthetize dolphins, they die. Not possessing involuntary respiratory mechanisms as humans do, dolphins must choose the time and place for each and every breath. And, while this may seem logical, given their aquatic surroundings, it represents a fundamental departure from the conventional mammalian norm.

Imagine how very different our lives would be if each breath we took was the result of a conscious effort. Aside from the obvious effects on sleeping habits and other behaviors, wouldn't the need to always choose to breathe require basic changes in the way we view life? Unable to take life for granted, we might be constantly reminded by each new breath of just how tenuous and fragile our existence is. By the same token, the rigorous necessity of returning to the surface for each breath

Dolphin. James D. Watt.

places a severe constraint on survival. In an environment that is generally hostile to mammalian life, unconsciousness, forgetfulness, and excessive fatigue would be fatal. It seems plausible that a species with this sort of constraint on its survival might have developed, through natural selection, a compensatory behavior; in this case, compassion—an allegedly unscientific term that most scientists are loathe to utilize in describing nonhuman species.

Species whose individuals and social groups assist one another in maintaining survival are actively

In 1988 biologist Samuel LaBudde documented the dolphin slaughter firsthand, and later the destructiveness of ocean driftnets. Thanks to the work of Samuel and Earth Island Institute most tuna is now "dolphin-safe."
Bahamas. Bob Talbot.

maximizing both their own chances for reproduction and the likelihood that the genes that encode "altruistic" behavior will be passed on to the next generation. This could explain why dolphins are a "compassionate" species who routinely assist their weak, ill, and injured kindred. It doesn't begin to explain, however, why they extend this assistance to other cetaceans, like whales, or to distinctly non-cetacean species, like humans.

Through history, dolphins have saved the lives of thousands of people from drowning and shark attacks; the question remains, why. Are they simply acting out of a genetically conditioned loyalty to large-brained mammalian life? Not likely, especially since we know that dolphins act of their own will. A dolphin's conscious process of recognizing that a human is in danger, realizing that it can act to remove that danger, and then acting to do just that, seems compelling enough argument for us humans to accede some of our selfish notions about intelligence and compassion to the dolphins. There is certainly nothing to suggest that dolphins save humans in order to increase their own chances of survival, particularly in light of our unrelenting slaughter of their populations. The only viable explanation for the dolphin behavior of showing concern for humans is that the dolphins care. Whether the dolphins' kindness toward humans is an innate or learned behavior, the fact remains that at least some of them feel that our survival as individuals is important.

With respect to the topic of intraspecies communication it should be noted that the dolphins have made their position very clear. It would be difficult, if not impossible, to think of a more profound or meaningful way of communicating than saving the life of another living being. It's about time that human beings begin communicating in return. To do that, it might be helpful to acknowledge that dolphins maybe aren't so much dolphins, as "dolphin beings," and that humanity is not a characteristic reserved for humans.

PHOTOGRAPHERS' BIOGRAPHIES

Brian Ansell, an Australian, has lived in Vanuatu, a small island republic in the southwest Pacific, for the past twenty-two years. He has dived in the Caribbean as well as off many Pacific islands and on the Great Barrier Reef. Previous works include a calendar, magazine articles, and postage stamps for Vanuatu.

Dr. Robert Ballard is a senior scientist at the Woods Hole Oceanographic Institution who specializes in advanced deep-water exploration technology. Dr. Ballard, along with his team, is credited with the discovery of the wreck of the *Titanic*. He received his Ph.D. from the University of Rhode Island in marine geology/physics.

Frank Balthis has a master's degree in environmental politics; he specializes in photographs of coastal scenes and marine mammals. He lives in Santa Cruz, California.

Robert E. Barber is a wildlife photographer and sculptor. His work has appeared in a variety of books, calendars, and magazines. He photographs both land and marine animals and lives in Arvada, Colorado.

Fred Bavendam specializes in behavioral aspects of marine life and life-cycle information and is noted for his sequential shots of mating, feeding, and other behavior in the marine world. A professional photographer for seven years, he has had cover shots and stories in *National Geographic* and *Smithsonian*, and his photos have also run in *Natural History*. He wrote and photographed *Beneath Cold Waters: The Marine Life of New England* (Down East Publishing). He spends eight to ten months a year traveling.

Michael Baytoff concentrates on nature and environmental issues. His work has appeared in *Audubon, Time, Newsweek, Aperture,* and *U.S. News & World Report,* and other magazines as well as in several books. He makes his home in Flemington, New Jersey.

Mark Conlin has been involved with two award-winning wildlife documentary films while working with Howard Hall Productions. *Seasons in the Sea* and *Shadows in a Desert Sea* each won the Golden Panda Award at the Wildscreen Film Festival. Conlin, who has a degree in marine biology, has had photos published in *International Wildlife, Ocean Realm, Terre Sauvage,* and *Natural History*.

Anne Doubilet wrote the children's book *Under the Sea from A to Z* (Crown). A graduate of Boston University, she earned her diving certificate in 1968 and took up marine photography in 1974. Her pictures have appeared in *National Geographic*. She is a freelance photographer/stock library editor, and she lives in New York City.

David Doubilet is the author of *Pacific: An Undersea Journey* (Bulfinch) and *Light in the Sea* (Thomasson-Grant).

Doubilet provided the photos for *Under the Sea from A to Z*, a children's book written by his wife, Anne. One of the chief photographers for *National Geographic*, he has won several awards from the National Press Photographers' Association and the University of Missouri School of Journalism. He is famous for his split-lens, over-water/under-water technique in shooting ocean scenes. He lives with his wife in New York City.

Dudley Foster is a senior pilot of the *Alvin* deep-sea submersible. He joined the *Alvin* group in 1972, and manages *Alvin*'s at-sea operations and crew. He has a B.S. in mechanical engineering from California State Polytechnical University.

Scott Frier, formerly chief expedition photographer for Jacques Cousteau, has been an underwater photographer for more than fifteen years. He was the principal photographer for Cousteau's books *Amazon Journey* and *Jacques Cousteau's Calypso*, and his work has appeared in *Time, Discover, Ocean Realm,* and numerous other magazines. He teaches underwater photography for Nikon. He specializes in fish portraiture and lives in Los Angeles, California.

Lynn Funkhouser is a frequently published photographer and active environmentalist. She is vice president of the International Marinelife Alliance, USA, and an advisory director to Ocean Voice International in Canada. She has received the Lifetime Achievement Award from the Philippine Aquatic and Marinelife Conservationists Association, Inc.

Jim Gritz, the photography editor of *Ocean*, is the director of Global Editions, a marine and wildlife greeting card company, and is also an accomplished marine photographer. His photography has received awards from the Art Directors Club of Denver, including a gold medal for his 1991 underwater calendar. He lives in Boulder, Colorado, where he also runs a photo stock company called Global Pictures.

Al Grotell has been a marine photographer for more than twenty years. His photos have appeared in such magazines as *Outside, Omni, Travel & Leisure,* and *Scientific American,* as well as in several books. He lives in New York City.

Howard Hall, a four-time Emmy Award winner for cinematography, is a natural history film producer specializing in underwater films. Hall is an associate editor for *Ocean Realm* magazine and a contributing editor for *International Wildlife*. His book *Howard Hall's Guide to Successful Underwater Photography* (Marcor Publishing) is in its fourth printing. Howard Hall Productions is based in Del Mar, California.

David Hall earned second place in the 1992 BBC Wildlife Photographer of the Year competition (underwater category). He is most interested in the interrelationships between animals found on coral reefs. His photos have appeared in 100 books, and in magazines such as *Natural History, Time, Ocean Realm, Audubon,* and *Omni*. He resides in Woodstock, New York.

Dr. Paul Hargraves is a professor of oceanography at the University of Rhode Island. He received a Ph.D. in marine science from the College of William and Mary and specializes in studying the taxonomy and distribution of marine phytoplankton. His pictures have appeared in several textbooks and publications, including *National Geographic*. He lives in Saunderstown, Rhode Island.

Richard Herrmann looks for dramatic behavioral shots, and his photos have appeared in *Ocean Realm, Outside,* and *San Diego,* among other publications. He was 1991 BBC Wildlife Photographer of the Year. He lives in Poway, California.

Roger Hess, a native Californian, has been a professional photographer since the 1970s. He is a two-term president of the Underwater Photographic Society. In 1986, he and a partner started the Seaview Scuba Diving Show, now one of the largest such shows in the United States. Hess lives in San Lorenzo, California.

Dr. Robert Hessler is a leader in the study of hydrothermal vent life. He is a professor of biological oceanography at the Scripps Institution of Oceanography at the University of California at San Diego. He received his Ph.D. in invertebrate paleontology from the University of Chicago in 1960.

Michio Hoshino is a Japanese-born photographer specializing in the wildlife of Alaska. His book *Grizzly* (Chronicle) won the Anima Award for distinguished wildlife photography, and several other books of his photography have been published. His work has appeared in *National Geographic*.

Burt Jones and Maurine Shimlock are based in landlocked Austin, Texas, but have traveled the world to take their award-winning marine photographs. Their marine portfolio was the runner-up for the grand prize in the 1991 BBC Wildlife Photographer of the Year competition and the highest-rated portfolio of exclusively underwater photographs. Their company Secret Sea Visions is "dedicated to using the art of photography to preserve the sea."

Alex Kerstitch is a photographer and scientist. As a scientist, he has discovered eight new species, including a shrimp called the *Chacella kerstitchi*, an olive snail called the *Oliva kerstitchi*, and a cone snail called the *Conus kerstitchi*. He was selected one of the five top underwater photographers in the nation in the October 1988 issue of *Natural History* and has twice won first-place awards in *Natural History* photographic competitions. He is a research associate at the University of Arizona in Tucson where he lives.

Alex Kirkbride grew up in London and now lives in New York City. He specializes in underwater photography, and his photographic interests also include people, wildlife, and travel adventure. Clients include *Travel & Leisure, Scuba Diving, British Journal of Photography, Ocean Realm,* and the ad firms McCann Erickson, and Young & Rubicam.

Frans Lanting does much of his work for *National Geographic,* for whom he is often on assignment shooting wildlife. A *terra firma* photographer, Lanting has done a great deal of work on the ecology of Africa. His penguin shots are featured in *The Total Penguin* (Prentice Hall). He won the BBC Wildlife Photographer of the Year award in 1991. He was born in Rotterdam and now lives near Monterey Bay in California.

Dr. Laurence P. Madin is an associate scientist at the Woods Hole Oceanographic Institution. He specializes in the biology of zooplankton as well as the study of tunicates, ctenophores, and other animals. He received his Ph.D. from the University of California, Davis, in zoology.

Dr. George Matsumoto is interested in the natural history, taxonomy, and behavior of all gelatinous zooplankton. He received his Ph.D. from UCLA in marine biology, and is now a post-doctoral scholar at Stanford University's Hopkins Marine Station on Monterey Bay. His photos have been published in numerous publications and his articles in several scientific journals.

Amos Nachoum won Nikon's 1988 international underwater photography contest and is an instructor on Nikon's team of photographers. He co-founded Israel's Marine National Park and also founded La Mer Diving Seafari, Inc., in New York. He has led several expeditions for *National Geographic,* and he co-produced two movies with Stan Waterman. His photos have appeared in *Condé Nast Traveler, Skin Diving,* and *Scuba Diving*.

Chris Newbert has won more than thirty awards in international underwater photographic competitions, and his writing and photographs grace his award-winning book *Within a Rainbowed Sea*. The *Los Angeles Times* said *Within a Rainbowed Sea* "has exhausted critics' superlatives...[It] has won more gold medals than Edwin Moses." The book is an official presidential gift of state given to foreign dignitaries. Newbert and his wife, Birgitte Wilms, founded Rainbowed Sea Tours, Inc., a dive travel company. Newbert is an associate editor for *Ocean Realm* magazine and lives in Basalt, Colorado.

Chuck Nicklin has been diving for forty years. He is an underwater cinematographer who has worked on such films as *The Abyss* and *For Your Eyes Only,* as well as numerous documentaries. He owns the Diving Locker in San Diego, California, with his son Terry and lives in La Jolla, California.

Flip Nicklin has been called the "premier whale photographer in the world" by the *Los Angeles Times*. He frequently shoots pictures of marine mammals for *National Geographic*. He began diving at the age of eleven, and he often free-dives when shooting whales because they are bothered by the bubbles produced by scuba equipment.

Doug Perrine's work has been published in more than 300 magazines and newspapers worldwide, including *U.S. News & World Report, Ocean Realm,* the *New York Times,* and *National Geographic Traveler*. He has a master's degree in biology from the University of Miami's School of Marine Science and has worked as a fisheries biologist for the National Marine Fisheries Service. He lives in Miami, Florida

Courtney Platt's work has been featured in *National Geographic, Time, Ocean Realm,* and *Forbes,* as well as in other magazines and books. As the captain of submersibles for Research Submersibles Limited from 1986 to 1988, Platt piloted numerous dives to 1,000 feet. He is a full-time professional photographer based in Grand Cayman.

Carl Roessler led a design team at Yale University in developing a time-sharing Management Information System before moving to the Caribbean. He has been interested in underwater photography since 1967. Roessler has amassed over 250,000 pictures of aquatic subjects, the world's largest private collection of underwater photos, and has created several books including *The Underwater Wilderness* (Chanticleer Press), *Coral Kingdoms* (Harry N. Abrams), and *Great Reefs of the World* (Gulf Publishing/Pisces). He is the president of See & Sea Travel, Inc., in San Francisco, California, where he also lives.

Steve Rosenberg is a professional writer/photographer and videographer based in northern California. He is interested in underwater photography, marine biology, advertising, and dive travel. Rosenberg has had four books published to date, including diving guides on Hawaii, northern California, and Cozumel as well as a text on shooting underwater video. He also has more than 250 articles and thousands of photographs in print, appearing in a variety of books, magazines, calendars, posters, and advertisements.

Kevin Schafer is a wildlife photographer whose work appears in all of the major nature and science magazines worldwide. Concentrating on tropical rain forests, he spends part of every year documenting the wildlife of Central and South America. When not overseas, he lives in New York City with his wife, writer Martha Hill.

Eric Schwarz has been photographing the marine life found in the cold waters of the North Atlantic for the last twenty-five years. His work has appeared in *Skin Diver* and *Underwater USA* and is currently being used by the Mystic (CT) Marinelife Aquarium.

Nancy Sefton is an award-winning nature photographer, residing in the Seattle, Washington, area. She is a widely published freelance writer on ocean-oriented subjects and has also produced an award-winning video documentary on coral reef ecology.

Marty Snyderman has published four books on marine wildlife. His photographs have appeared in *National Geographic, Natural History, Audubon, Newsweek,* and other magazines. He specializes in shooting large, rare, and potentially dangerous marine life. He lives in San Diego, California.

Kevin and Cat Sweeney, of the big island of Hawaii, specialize in nature photography of the underwater environment. As freelance photojournalists, they have been published worldwide in numerous magazines and calendars.

Bob Talbot has created more than thirty marine mammal posters, and his photos have been published in such magazines as *Audubon, Omni, American Photographer, Natural History,* and *Ocean Realm.* He is also a cinematographer who has worked on Cousteau Society productions as well as programs for network television.

Wes Walker is a superior court judge in Napa, California. His photos have been published in *Sierra, Defenders, Weekly Reader,* and the *London Sunday Times,* among others, and have been used by Greenpeace and the Senate Finance Committee in connection with drift net legislation. He concentrates on environmental issues and wildlife scenes.

James D. Watt gave up a career as a medical technician ten years ago to become a marine photographer. He now specializes in large marine animals such as whales, dolphins, and sharks. His photographs have appeared in more than 300 magazines, including *National Geographic, International Wildlife,* and *Smithsonian.* A native of Los Angeles, Watt now lives in Kailua-Kona, Hawaii, with his family.

F. Stuart Westmorland is a full-time travel stock photographer based in Seattle, Washington. His images appear regularly in a variety of travel and underwater publications, aquarium displays, advertising campaigns, calendars, and postcards.

Thomas Wiewandt is an author, photographer, cinematographer, and scientist. He wrote and photographed *Hidden Life of the Desert* (Crown) and has done films for the BBC and the National Geographic Society. He has a Ph.D. in ecology and a master's degree in photography. He lives in Tucson, Arizona.

Birgitte Wilms, formerly an underwater model, has moved behind the lens as an underwater photographer. The Danish-born Wilms's work has been featured in numerous European publications, *Ocean Realm,* and *Islands,* and she won Best of Show in the first contest she ever entered, the 17th Annual Underwater Photographic Society International Competition in Los Angeles. She lives in Basalt, Colorado, with her husband, Chris Newbert, and is vice president of Rainbowed Sea Tours, Inc.

Norbert Wu is the author and photographer of *Life in the Oceans* (Little, Brown) and *Beneath the Waves* (Chronicle). He won first place in the 1987 Nikon International photo contest. According to *Nature Photographer* magazine, "Wu has risen to the top of his profession." He has also filmed documentaries for PBS and ABC. He lives in Orinda, California.

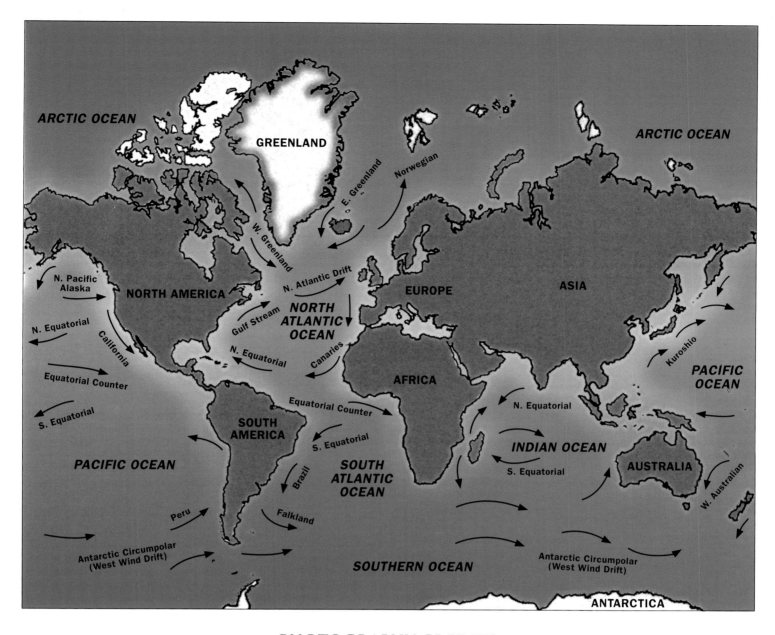

PHOTOGRAPHY CREDITS

INDEX